60

76

AN IMPRESSIVE RENAISSANCE TOWN —

"Torgau's buildings are more beautiful than all those of the ancient world; even Solomon's Temple was only made of wood."

MARTIN LUTHER

Dear reader,

Today, Torgau is undoubtedly one of the most important towns in Saxony that are associated with Martin Luther. This town, where the traces of the Reformation are omnipresent, is a jewel of German Renaissance architecture that has hardly changed in the last 500 years. A special treat is the view of Torgau from the banks of the river Elbe. When walking through the town taking in the sights, you are still treading the same lanes that Martin Luther, Philipp Melanchthon, Georg Spalatin and Gabriel Didymus passed on their way to Hartenfels Castle. Here, their sovereign resided: Elector Frederick the Wise – and after him his successors, John the Steadfast and John Frederick the Magnanimous from the House of Wettin. They were supporters of Luther's and his actions and granted him political backing, which is why contemporary witnesses call Wittenberg the mother and Torgau the nursemaid of the Reformation. In any case, Torgau was the political centre of the Reformation in Germany. It was here where alliances for the protection of the new religion were forged, and with the "Articles of Torgau" an important foundation of the Augsburg Confession was made, which is still the primary confession in the Evangelical-Lutheran Church today.

Let Torgau invite you to visit authentic Reformation sites. Discover a vivid town with cultural traditions connected to the work of the composers Johann Walter and Heinrich Schütz. The Castle Chapel was the first new construction of a Protestant church ever made and was consecrated in 1544 by Martin Luther himself. Its programmatically plain architecture represents the renewed faith. With the castle and Castle Chapel as main attractions, our city is currently applying for recognition as world heritage. In the town church "St. Marien" you can visit Katharina von Bora's grave. The Katharina Luther Parlour houses an exhibition to commemorate the work of the courageous woman at Luther's side. Come and have a look at the interesting special exhibitions at the castle or follow the unique Torgau Museum Path.

Welcome to Torgau and North Saxony. I hope you will enjoy this interesting read.

Andrea Staude
Mayor of Torgau

Contents

◄ Cover picture
Hartenfels Castle along with the Wendelstein and the Watchman Tower

THE POLITICAL CENTRE OF THE REFORMATION — *Hartenfels Castle was the residence of the Electors from the Ernestine branch of the House of Wettin. On numerous occasions, the political course for the Reformation in Electoral Saxony and in the whole Empire was set here.*

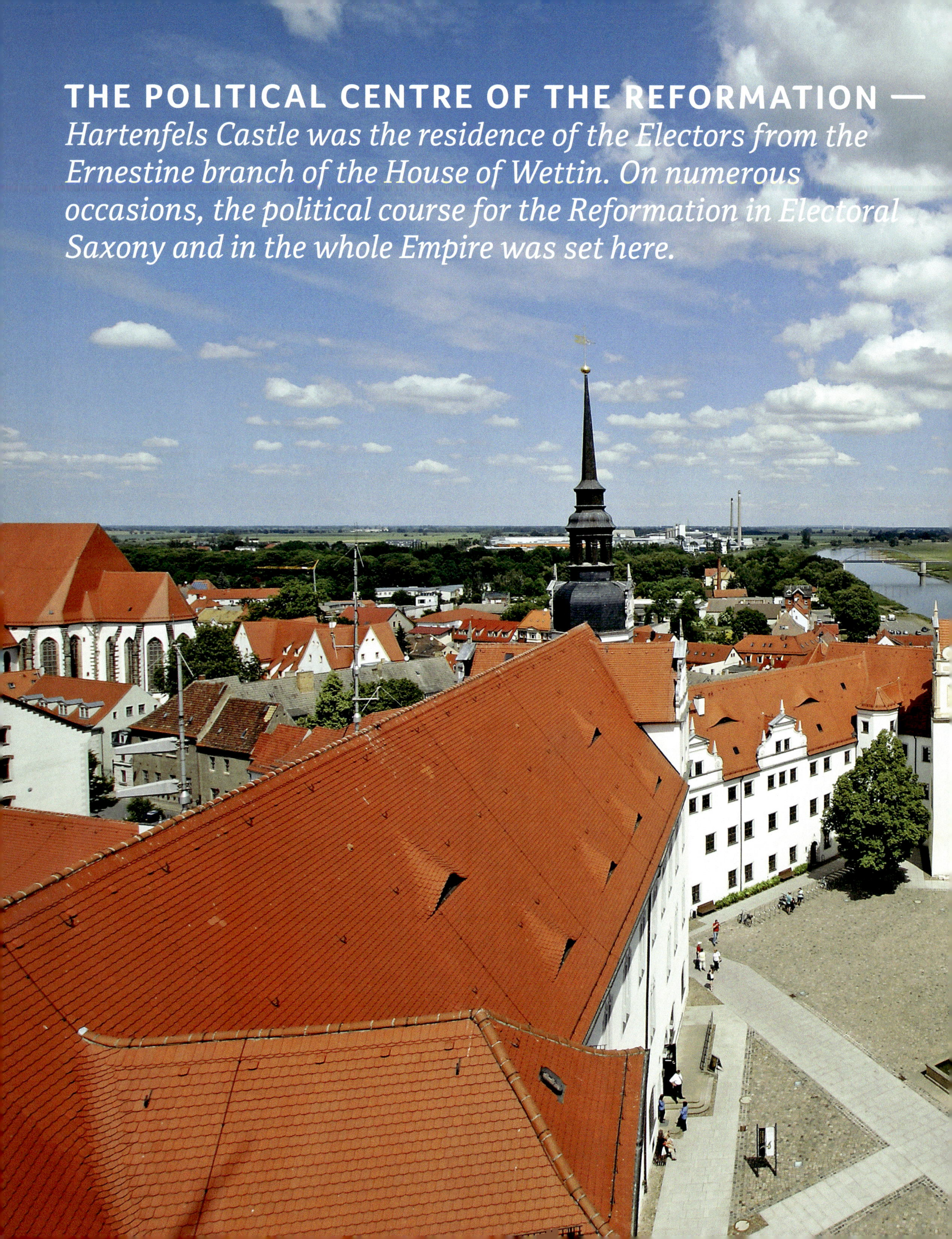

APOTHEKE
Deutsche Bank
Deutsche Bank
HOTEL
GOLDENER ANKER
ZIMMER

A VERY SPECIAL ENSEMBLE OF MONUMENTS —

More than 500 very well-preserved late Gothic, Renaissance and Baroque as well as Neoclassical and Art Nouveau buildings create a unique historical townscape. The thousand-year-old town has been a heritage area since 1979.

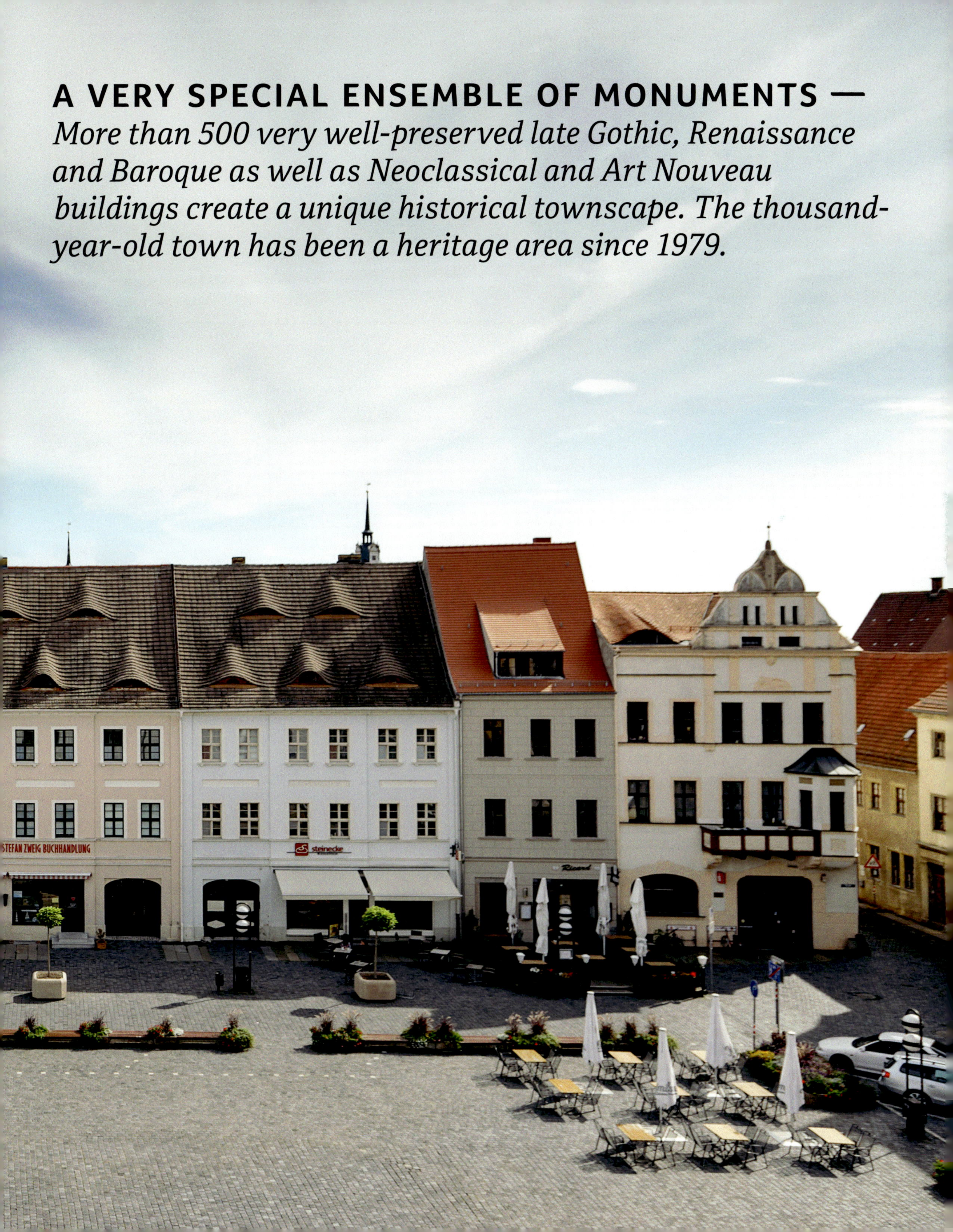

Discover Torgau

BY JÜRGEN HERZOG AND KATHRIN NIESE

Beer – the Town's Bread

Torgau was famous for its beer, which was the town's bread. It was much praised for its quality, but it also was the centre of many people's everyday life: that of the council, the brewers, the many helpers, indeed the entire brewing family and, most of all, that of the women. In the 16th century, Torgau was the most important beer producer in Saxony. About ten thousand barrels a year left the town by land and water. Those who were allowed to brew large amounts were wealthy. The great houses in the historic town centre, with their fermentation and storage cellars carved deep into the rocks, bear witness to this until today. Wolf Giersing, the tax collector of the office in Lautern Petersberg, invested in a bourgeois house in Torgau: a brewery that was allowed to brew about 30,000 litres of beer per year. What is now the Torgauer Braumuseum (brewing museum) was at the time his provision for old age, and its medieval cellar-vaults and barroom still reflect the old times, when beer was "the town's bread".

▶ www.museum-torgau.de

The House Behind the "Bäckerwall" – Historic Workman House

People wanted to live and work well protected within the town walls and moats. But not too close to the wall, where the air was smelly, the lanes were not cobbled and no water ran. Bent with the weight of generations, today's "Handwerkerhaus" (Workman House) stands here. However, it had only been inhabited by workmen in the 17th century: coopers, who had to make the barrels for the town's famous beer, and chimney sweepers, who climbed up and down the flues. They were succeeded by the poorest: night guards, brewers, servants and transport workers, who often had many children.

Come and experience the narrow, simple living conditions offered by this tiny house, in which even the least bit of space was used – and, of course, the surprisingly witty mural paintings, which make a deep impact.

▶ www.museum-torgau.de

Kingly Splendour at Paul Ringenhain's

A band of forty angels are floating at the ceiling, playing music or carrying the Weapons of Christ. The hunting lounge is decorated with plenty of animals, among them, of course, an aurochs protected by armed guards. In such splendour lived Mayor Paul Ringenhain. He was Torgau's richest citizen of his day. He had his stately Renaissance house built in 1596, and due to his lifelong ambition to furnish it ever more wealthily, kingly splendour entered the bourgeois milieu. The angel room mentioned above was modelled on an identical room at Hartenfels Castle, which is lost, unfortunately. The beautiful original furniture of this bourgeois house allows the visitor to reminisce about the cultural life of a wealthy family at the turn of the 17th century.

▶ www.museum-torgau.de

Carl Loebner Enterprise – Germany's Oldest Toy Store

One of the many attractions of Torgau is Germany's oldest toy store, which the Loebner family have owned for more than 300 years. Wood turner Christoph Loebner started his workshop in Torgau as early as 1685, and principally made spin tops, rattles and simple dolls from wood or horn. In 1780, the Loebner family bought the house at No. 2, Bäckerstraße, near the Town Hall, where the store is still located today. By now, the traditional family business is run by the eleventh generation. Since 2006, the Loebner family's large collection of toys is at display at the museum of cultural and town history "Stadt- und Kulturgeschichtliches Museum Torgau".

▶ www.spielwaren-carl-loebner.de

▶ **DR JÜRGEN HERZOG**
is a historian and the president of the Torgau History Association.

▶ **KATHRIN NIESE**
is a museologist and works at the "Stadt- und Kulturgeschichtliche Museum".

TOUR OF THE TOWN

Winding lanes, small gardens, romantic corners – and the town church St. Marien towering above all, resting in itself. Thousand-year-old Torgau, the northernmost town of the Free State of Saxony, attracts visitors and invites them to explore. Follow the track of electors and reformers ...

Torgau as Reflected at Reformation Times

A tour of the historic centre on the track of Martin Luther

BY HANS-JOACHIM KADATZ

The impressive entire complex of Hartenfels Castle at break of day

(1) The starting point of the tour is Hartenfels Castle, which now houses the administrative office of North Saxony. The medieval castle complex, arisen from a former border post of the Margraviate of Meissen, began its transformation to a modern residential castle in 1485, following the ideas of Italian and French palace building.

As he used to be received in audience by the Elector and to preach at the chapel called "Martinskapelle", which existed until 1533, the Reformer doubtlessly belonged to the admirers of the splendid Early Renaissance wings that were built back then. They were dominated by the statically ingenious "Wendelstein", a spiral staircase carved in stone, created by Conrad Krebs between 1533 and 1536. After Krebs' death, the Thuringian Nickel Gromann continued with the construction of the adjacent wing that houses the electoral chambers, to which the Elector had the Castle Chapel directly adjusted. In this prototype of Protestant sacred buildings, constructed from 1543 to 1544, Luther's conceptual ideas were put into practice for the first time. The rich interior furnishing was designed by the sculptors Simon Schröter the Elder from Torgau and Stephan Hermsdorf from Leipzig and Freiberg, as well as master Lucas Cranach the Elder from Wittenberg. The so-called Little Masters, like Peter Flötner, brought in some special decorative details.

It is well worth climbing the 53-metres-high Watchman Tower (the highest tower of the castle)

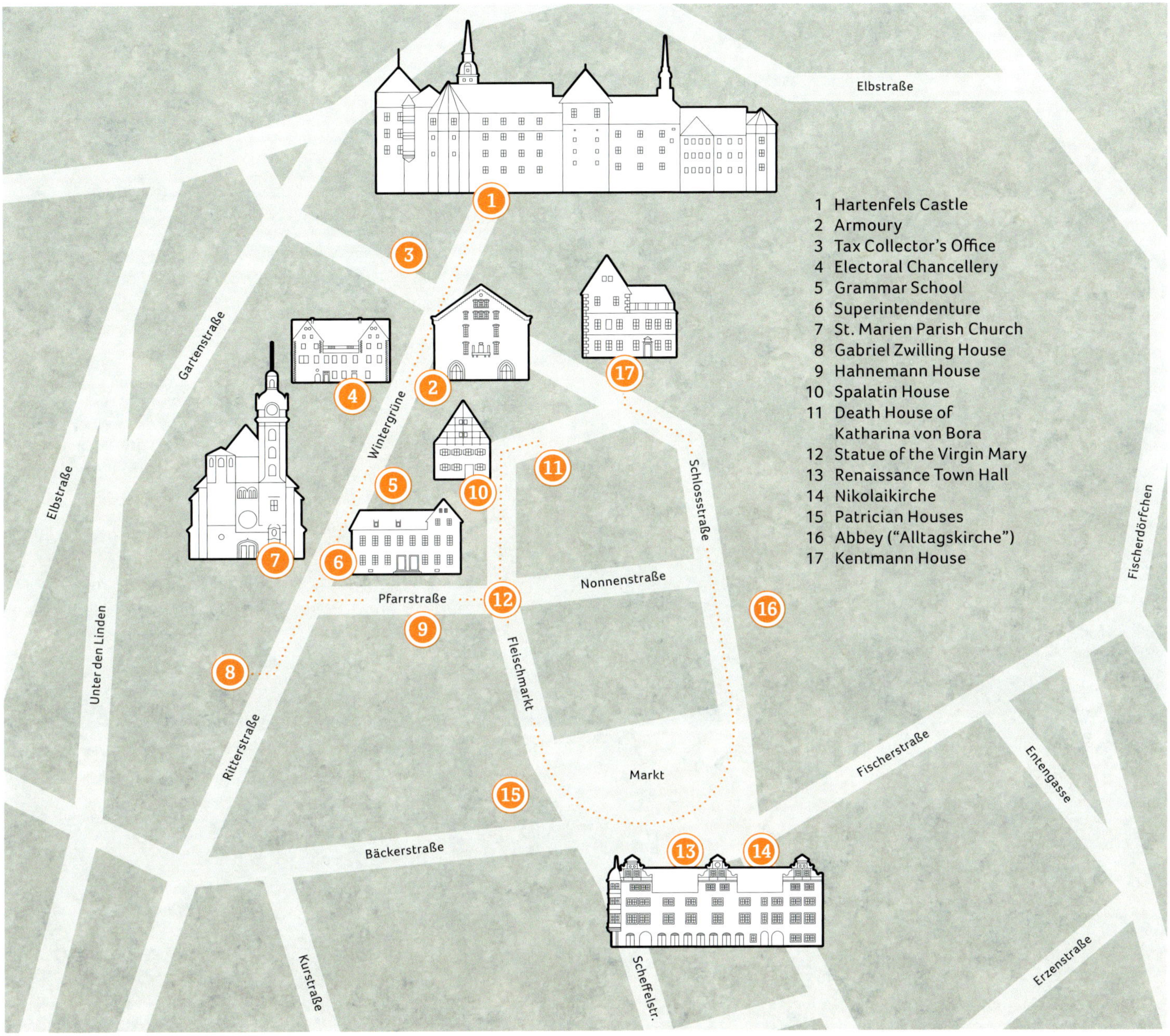

to enjoy the views of the interior courtyard and the town set in the surrounding landscape of the Elbe Lowlands. From this tower, the view over the river course reveals all the special associations with the historic events that took place in the former Margraviate of Meissen.

(2) The monumental Armoury at the castle courtyard was a late Gothic granary in 1479. From 1538 onwards, it housed the royal stables, and after the changes of the 18th and 19th centuries it served as a Prussian armoury. In 1999, the "Heimerer Schulen", a group of educational institutions for social care, set up one of their schools in this house.

(3) The "Wintergrüne" (wintergreen), a somewhat mysterious street name of the former "Burgfreiheit", a walled residential area in the oldest part of the settlement, is bounded by the wings of the old casting house and of the Tax Collector's Office behind the bear moat (▶ p. 19). The Tax Collector's Office was first mentioned in 1462. Like the castle's facades, these wings were robbed of their beauty at the time when the construction was used as Prussian barracks. The most important passage between the two buildings has been leading through the oldest town wall and over the "Schlosstorbrücke" (castle gate bridge) to the former moorings and ship mills on the banks of the river Elbe since the 13th/14th century.

At the Superintendenture, the "Articles of Torgau", written by the reformers around Martin Luther, paved the way for the Augsburg Confession of 1530.

▲
Back of the Chancellery at No. 5, Wintergrüne. This building used to be the former electoral administration office, today it houses the "Stadt- und Kulturgeschichtliche Museum"

4 On the grounds of No. 5, Wintergrüne, a former farmyard of the Cistercian nuns of Nimbschen, the Elector had the Electoral Chancellery built as an amplified administration office parallel to the construction of the castle from 1523 onwards. The name "Electoral Chancellery" was first used in 1531.

A chancellor and eleven councillors were responsible for the execution of important documents and the implementation of the chancellery language of Saxony, into which Luther also translated the Bible. In the 18th century, one of the largest Saxon cloth manufactories was established here, in which Peter the Great and philosopher Leibniz met in 1711, among other things. In 2005, the museum of cultural and town history "Stadt- und Kulturgeschichtliches Museum Torgau" opened its doors for the first time.

5 In the court area of No. 6, Wintergrüne, the famous Torgau Grammar School has been standing since before 1371. This school was relocated later at the vacant Franciscan monastery under the reign of Maurice, Elector of Saxony. Here, brilliant humanists like the magisters and principals Corbusanius, Peucer, Böhme and Marcus Crodel, imparted antique literature and languages. Cantors like Conrad Rupsch and Johann Walter laid the foundation for Protestant choir music.

When Torgau became a fortress in 1883, the building's old structure was lost, except for a portal in the driveway, through which the Reformer himself may have passed when his oldest son Johannes, one of his nephews and one of Melanchthon's sons studied here from 1542 to 1543.

6 Only a few meters away lies the legendary Superintendenture at No. 2, Wintergrüne. The massive gabled corner house was being used as parish office of the Protestant church since 1525, and in 1529 it became the office of Gabriel Zwilling (referred to as Didymus), who at Luther's recommendation became the first superintendent of Torgau, and his successors. This house was the centre of the Reformation in Torgau, especially when Luther, Melanchthon, Jonas and Bugenhagen, on behalf of Elector John, worked out the final version of the "Articles of Torgau" in March 1530, which would become the basis of the Augsburg Confession.

7 The Superintendenture is located at the doorstep of St. Marien Parish Church (▶ p. 63). Built closely to the precipice of the oldest town walls and situated on one of the highest stretches of the historic town, it can be seen from a distance towering like a crown over the town. A part of the western front of the Romanesque basilica, which was first testified as early as 1119, is still intact today. Between 1450 and 1490, the much bigger nave of this

View of the St. Marien town church, Torgau's oldest church. The Gothic hall church built in the 15th century had a predecessor building testified as early as 1119

early Upper Saxon hall church that was finished around 1520 by master builder Hans of Torgau (also called Hans Meltwitz), was constructed due to the growth of the town. Apart from the spacious interior, the grave of Electress Sophie of Mecklenburg, the precious altarpiece picturing the "Fourteen Holy Helpers" by Lucas Cranach the Elder and the naturalistically designed gravestone of Katharina von Bora impress the visitor.

8 The church's main entrance allows a direct view of the building at No. 13, Ritterstraße, which was altered in the 17th century and has been housing the Gabriel Zwilling House (▶ p. 52) since 1540. With the endorsement of Georg Spalatin, Luther had initially recommended the former Augustinian monk and old friend as preacher of the Nikolaikirche and St. Marien, later he became superintendent after the visitation of Torgau.

9 In between lies the old free farmyard at No. 3, Pfarrstraße, which was in possession of Georg von Minkwitz around 1533. He was the Elector's counsellor and private tutor and was also involved in Reformation affairs.

In his Gothic gabled house, valuable traces of decorative paintings were found and preserved in 1991. Later in history, the building was renamed Hahnemann House after the homoeopath Samuel Hahnemann, who owned it from 1805 to 1811.

10 A quick side trip to Katharinenstraße, previously called Lutherstraße, might result in a stop at "Herr Käthe" inn. Just a few steps further you come upon the modest Spalatin House (▶ p. 46), which is currently being professionally reconstructed as a monument. Elector Frederick the Wise assigned it to his court chaplain, royal tutor, diplomat, private secretary and Reformation pioneer. In 1527 Luther, too, found temporary lodging here.

11 Not far away is No. 11, the Death House of Katharina von Bora (▶ p. 50), where she found housing and care after her serious travel accident on her flight from the plague in Wittenberg in summer 1552, until she died on the 20th December of the same year. The exhibition at the "Katharina Luther Parlour" has been dedicated to her life and fate since 1996.

12 After a short way back we discover the copy of a life-size Statue of the Virgin Mary at the facade of the upper floor of the corner house at No. 5, Fleischmarkt. As it marks the southern continuation of "Pfarrstraße" as "Nonnenstraße" (nun street), this copy is often referred to as "nun". The "Nunnengang" (nun passage) was the passageway between the Franciscan monastery and the former house of the Cistercian nuns outside the town walls.

13 After 1514, when a charter by Holy Roman Emperor Maximilian I strengthened Torgau's trade functions even further, the "new town" of the merchants, tradesmen and grocers developed quickly at

At the corner house at No. 5, Fleischmarkt, is a copy of a statue, often referred to as "nun". The original, a Virgin Annunciate, can be seen at St. Marien church

◀ P. 18
The Fountain of Neptune in the castle courtyard with the "beautiful oriel", behind which the elector's private rooms are located

The Bear Moat

No visitor of whatever age can escape the Torgau Bear Moat in front of Hartenfels Castle. The chronicles of the chequered history of bear keeping at the game enclosure of the electoral castle date back to the 15th century. In the mid-fifties of the previous century, some committed citizens rebuilt the enclosure in the course of the "Nationale Aufbauwerk" (the reconstruction project of the GDR) within 5,000 voluntary working hours. Since 2013 it is being renovated step by step.

▶ www.torgauer-baeren.de

kolibri

The Renaissance Town Hall from 1563. A prestigious construction of a confident Town Council, built by Valten Wegern from Dresden. It still is the town's administration office today

◄ P. 20
The Town Hall with the oriel from 1579. The hemispheric breastworks pay homage to Elector Augustus and his wife Anne of Denmark

the doorsteps of the ancient town. Now, the large market square became the centre of daily life, and it still is a popular spot for social events today. At the end of the 15th century, the area was still used as farmland, but the town cemetery was more and more displaced by development. On the premises of No. 5/6, Markt, at the corner of the Renaissance market square rose the old Gothic town hall, first mentioned in 1373. Luther frequently met the councillors here, before the building was taken down. In the popular bar room he enjoyed his much-valued "Torgisch Bier". From 1563 onwards, the Renaissance Town Hall arose, dominating the market square. The characteristic example of Upper Saxon architecture by architects from Torgau and Dresden with new ground plan and space solutions is crowned with the style-defining Dutch gables of the strung-together dormers. In 1577, the magnificent oriel at the market square was built, alongside the famous "Trinkstubenanbau" (bar room annexe) at Leipziger Straße. Its decorative theme pays homage to Elector Augustus I, who had presented himself as a special patron of the Town Hall's construction.

Torgau's unique architecture attests to the advanced public spirit of its citizens.

(14) The dominant of this former suburban area of the merchants' settlement was the Nikolaikirche, a late Romanesque pillar basilica built approximately between 1220 and 1250. It is the town's second oldest, subordinated parish and sermon church. It was a main gathering point of the supporters of anti-papism in pre-Reformation times, which was emphasised in 1519 and 1520 by the first German-language baptism and the first Protestant-style sermon. After the visitation of Torgau in 1529, the Council used the secularised building as linen and cloth hall. In 1565, the choir of the market church that was by then used as a multipurpose building was directly integrated into the back facade of the currently finished new Town Hall. The choir was

destroyed at a later date. Some further townly functions and architectural changes left behind but a torso of this important monument, still awaiting its cultural rebirth in the Town Hall's courtyard.

15 Several impressive Patrician Houses with facades with high windowed gables rival with one another at No. 3 and 4, Markt ("Mohrenapotheke" – a pharmacy), and on Scheffelstraße and Bäckerstraße. Remarkably enough, they are all within sight of each other, consciously symbolising upper-class authority over the Council's office. Other buildings that were structurally overdone later on have, in most cases, lost their charisma.

16 Now our way leads us down Schlossstraße to the Franciscan Abbey on the premises of the Johann-Walter-Gymnasium (a secondary school). The towerless late Gothic hall was built between 1484 and 1515 by Hans Meltwitz, concurrently with the completion of St. Marien. It replaced the former monastery church of 1243. After having been closed subsequently to the "Torgauer Klostersturm" (storming on the monastery) in 1525, it could be re-consecrated in 1529 as a Protestant church. It was, of course, used in many different ways over the centuries, until it eventually was inaugurated as the school hall of the Johann-Walter-Gymnasium in 1997 (▶ p. 28).

17 At the end of Schlossstraße and, indeed, of our tour we come across the Kentmann House and the historical tavern "Bärenschenke" in front of the entrance of the castle's rosery (▶ p. 58). Since 1566, the highly educated town physician Dr Johann Kentmann had been occupied with varied scientific publications on minerals, stocks of animals and plants and buildings in the area of Meissen. His proud gabled corner house along with its herbarium is one of the well-preserved examples of Upper German urban Renaissance farm houses.

From the beginning of the 19th century, Torgau's development to a fortress and Prussian garrison town was affected by a long period of urban restructuring; modern extensions were not made until the turn of the 20th century. ●

▶ **PROF DR DR HANS-JOACHIM KADATZ**
is a historian for architecture and town planning, and also the author of numerous publications on Germany's history of architecture and art.

The residence of the town physician and natural scientist Johann Kentmann (1518–1574) near the castle is probably one of the town's most beautiful secular buildings

◄
Renaissance houses of the 16th century on the eastern side of the market square and the pharmacy "Mohrenapotheke". The construction of the Town Hall brought along a prestigious development of the rest of the area with upper-class merchant and residential houses

◄ P. 22
The Franciscan abbey became the "Alltagskirche" for daily masses after the Reformation. Today the nave is used as school hall by the Johann-Walter-Gymnasium

The History of the Fortress of Torgau

A town's special fate

BY UWE NIEDERSEN

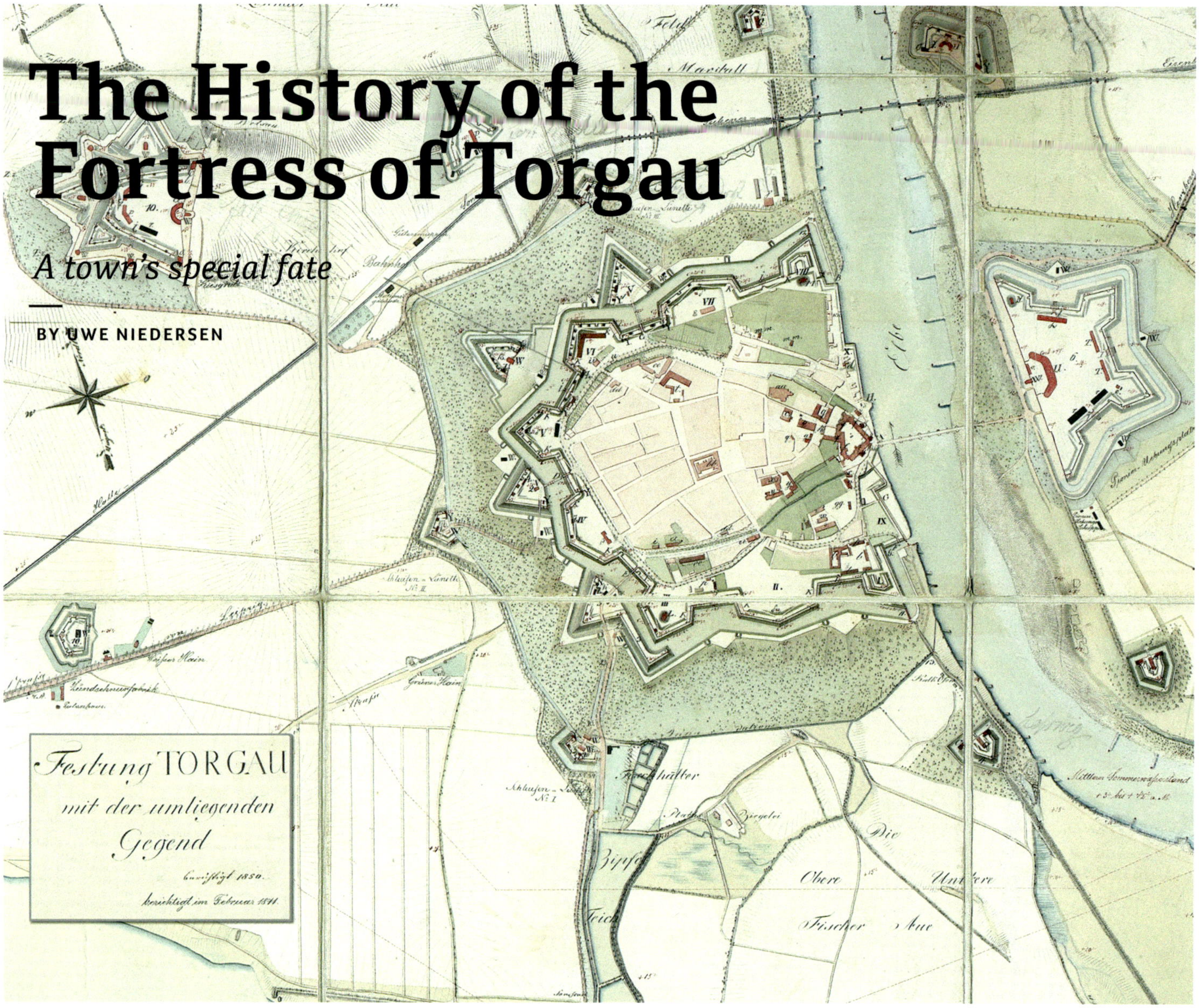

The fortress of Torgau around 1850, showing the main fortress with eight bastions and ravelins, the bridgehead, Fort Zinna, the "Neue Werk", Lunette Mahla as well as three water gate and Elbe lunettes

At the time of Elector Frederick the Wise around 1500, Torgau was surrounded by a zwinger. Leftovers of the drystone zwinger walls with crenels, turrets, but also rectangular wall projections and wet moats are still visible today in the areas of the castle, the Chancellery and the town church. Because of its increasing economic and political importance as well as the geostrategic location at the Middle Elbe, Torgau needed a town fortification supported by a bridgehead, i.e. a fortification at a defendable river crossing on the enemy side.

In 1531, Torgau wanted to establish a fortification "that has never been seen in the whole country before" on an edict of Elector John the Steadfast. The plans included an at the time modern fortification with bastions and vaulted dugouts for the soldiers. However, because of the sudden death of Elector John after a hunting accident in 1532, they were never put into practice. A new ordinance on the fortification of Torgau was not enacted by his son and successor John Frederick until the beginning of the Schmalkaldic War in 1546. But finances were short, which is why the Elector turned towards Wittenberg in the end, which already was a fully developed fortress of Electoral Saxony at the time. Consequently, John Frederick tried to reach the fortress of Wittenberg when the battle against the Imperial forces turned to his detriment on 24th April 1547, as Torgau, although very close to the battlefield, was not developed enough as a place of refuge.

The Albertine Duke Maurice, who was fighting for Emperor Charles V, spared the town. After John Frederick's capture and loss of power, he surely had no intention to have Torgau sacked by the Imperial troops, as he wanted to establish his own residence there as well.

During the Thirty Years' War, the Saxon architect Johann Wilhelm Dilich constructed the fortress of Torgau. He built his entrenchment lines in Dutch style: flat earth walls and wide, but at the same time deep trenches. About 100 years later, the structures of the fortifications in and around Torgau would again become subject to fundamental reconstruction. A permanent crossing over the river Elbe, routes of transportation by water and land in general, as well as magazines and military hospitals were essential in the Seven Years' War (1756–1763).

A military strategic situation like this needed a modern fortress, for the construction of which the Prussian King Frederick II himself and his fortress architect Simon L. Lefèbvre were responsible.

Now, let's have a look at the beginning of the following century. After Saxony had lost the battle of Jena-Auerstedt alongside with Prussia in 1806, the Saxons allied with Napoleon. The Elector of Saxony Frederick Augustus became King, but Saxony was principally lacking a central military training area. And so Torgau became a Saxon fortress at the river Elbe. Round 1810, the Saxon engineering officers planned to set up a belt of entrenchments and outworks around the actual main fortress. Between this outer ring and the defensive enclosure of the main fortress existed an "entrenched camp", where thousands of Saxon soldiers who were allied with the main fortress would find a place of assembly and refuge, from where they could take either offensive or defensive actions.

Napoleon I in his coronation robes, 1810, adapted from a painting by François Gérard

For Napoleon I, the setup of the Saxon fortress of Torgau at the river Elbe had a different function, of course. He needed a campaign fortress at the Middle Elbe for his deployment to Russia in 1812.

The new function of the fortress now consisted in ensuring the mobility of the Napoleonic troops. The construction of this campaign fortress brought about a shortening of the outer wall, resulting in the evacuation of the citizens of the western suburbs, the teardown of their houses, churches, hospitals and orphanage alike, as well as the closure of the cemetery.

The construction of the town's protective fortifications was very chequered indeed.

The gorge defence of the bridgehead. Gorge moat defence and defensive wall with loopholes and the imposing building of the defence barracks

After the Russian campaign had failed, the Saxon general August Freiherr von Thielmann became commander of the fortress of Torgau in 1813. He was attached to the Wars of Liberation and the "German cause". The citizens of French-held Wittenberg sent out an appeal for help in the form of an "Open Letter from the Town, Fortress and University of Wittenberg to the Royal Saxon Lieutenant General von Thielmann in Torgau" (excerpt):

"Dear neighbour full of grace.
Yours is our praise;
oh come to help the Saxon town!
From the chains set us free,
and help us to flee;
Think of late Luther and me!"

Of course Luther's town could not be helped immediately. It was not freed from French occupation until the beginning of 1814.

Meanwhile, a typhus epidemic spread in Torgau in 1813. The small fortress was absolutely unable to cope with the transfer of the French military hospitals. "How many mourning widows and helpless orphans may Torgau possess?" asked Friedrich Joseph Grulich in 1814. Today we know the answer: Nearly 30,000 people died in Torgau, among them far more than 1,000 citizens of the town.

After the Congress of Vienna of 1815, two thirds of the territory of Electoral Saxony were attributed to Prussia. Suddenly Torgau was a fortress on the border to Saxony, and in its further development became a Prussian garrison and bureaucratic town. The industrial development that proceeded in other towns could impossibly take place at the same level in Torgau, because of the spatial restrictions set by the fortress. This is why the historic town can still be experienced in such a vivid, charming way today. By the bye, during its entire time as a Prussian fortress (1815–1889), not a single cannon shot was fired from Torgau. However, the mere existence of the fortress was criticised by some sceptical people even back then. One of them was the archdeacon of the town's Protestant consecration, Johann Christian August Bürger, who appealed to the citizens' (Christian) conscience, claiming that the constant and everlasting did not lie within the colossus called "fortress". The churchman quoted Luther when he called out: "A [really] mighty fortress is our God!" In 1889, the fortress of Torgau was razed, and our town's time as a fortress over.

What is left is the history of the fortress of Torgau and the monuments of the fortifications from that time, which can still be seen today. All the well-preserved elements of fortification, like the bridgehead, the lunettes at the river Elbe, Fort Zinna, the war powder magazines, posterns, hollow traverses, flank casemates, and many more are described in the author's publication "Führungen durch die Festung Torgau" (Tours of the Fortress of Torgau) from 2011 in a clear and comprehensible way. ●

▶ **DR UWE NIEDERSEN**
is a historian who has published numerous works on the philosophy and history of science as well as on the history of Torgau; Förderverein Europa Begegnungen e. V.

Christian Wolff (editor)
Thomas Church in Leipzig
Church guide
64 pages | Paperback
ISBN 978-3-374-02190-1

€ 6,80 [D]

St. Thomas Church in Leipzig is one of Germany's most outstanding sacred buildings and is full of tradition. Johann Sebastian Bach, who is buried in the church's choir made this place of worship well-known and a fascinating spot for visitors from all over the world.

Clearly arranged and richly illustrated, this guide offers english speaking readers all that is interesting to know about St. Thomas Church:

- Building and construction history
- Personalities linked to St. Thomas Church
- Organs and other instruments in St. Thomas Church
- The St. Thomas Choir in the past and today and its most famous Thomaskantor Johann Sebastian Bach

Stiftung Frauenkirche Dresden
Frauenkirche Dresden
Church guide
64 pages | Paperback
ISBN 978-3-374-02335-6

SPECIAL REDUCED PRICE

€ 3,00 [D]

As the most significant domed building north of the Alps and a landmark of Protestant church architecture, the Dresden Frauenkirche is among the most important works of European cultural and architectural history.

This guide offers all the important facts about the Dresden Frauenkirche:

- The Church and its Construction History
- The Interior
- The Bells
- The Lower Church
- The Frauenkirche as an Open House of God and Man
- Events and Dates at a Glance

The Johann-Walter-Gymnasium in Torgau

A monastery turned into a school – an educational institution with tradition

BY HELMUT GRAUL

Located between the market square and Hartenfels Castle is one of Saxony's oldest establishments of higher education. Behind the abbey of the former Franciscan monastery are the new and annex buildings as well as the older building of the Johann-Walter-Gymnasium. The constructional ensemble is considered to be remarkably well-made from an architectonic point of view. However, its exact date of foundation is unknown. A deed of foundation of 1371 in which pupils are mentioned does exist in the town archives, but a school must have been there much earlier than that. It was located directly beside the town church "St. Marien" on the street Wintergrüne. Martin Luther's oldest son was registered in the pupil listing of the "Grammar School" in 1542. However, in the late 19th century the school's old building structure had to make way for the extension of the fortifications.

In the abbey of the Franciscan monastery, which had been built between 1485 and 1513, Protestant masses had been held since 1529, after the monks had left Torgau. Apart from its function as a church for daily service, it was used for several other purposes throughout the centuries: In the different wars during and after Torgau's time as a fortress, it was used as military hospital, barracks, armoury and garrison church; after 1933 it became a "National Socialist temple", in the former GDR it was called "Bernhard-Kellermann-Halle" and served as a theatre hall; and finally it served as a gym until 1995. During the pre-examinations preceding its renovation as a school hall, the word "Martinus" was found on the inside, written on the northern wall. The restorers consider it to be a direct pointer to Martin Luther.

The history of the other monastery buildings is similarly varied. When Wittenberg was plague-ridden in the mid-16th century, the university was relocated to the former monastery buildings. At that time, Philipp Melanchthon, who had drafted the fourth set of school regulations which was enacted in August 1531, lived in one of the annexes.

Doubtlessly, the school's most important tutor was Johann Walter (▶ p. 48), who taught here from 1529 to 1548. In 1524, the close friend and musical adviser of Luther had issued the "Geystliche

The renovated abbey, which now serves as school hall, and houses concerts, exhibitions, conferences, and also examinations

gesangk Buchleyn" (a choir book) in Wittenberg, and had directed the electoral choir of the Electoral Saxon residence of Torgau since 1526. Here in Torgau he founded the first Protestant boys' choir, which was closely linked to the school until the 1950s and sang in Torgau as well as on international concert tours. Around 1550, Johann Walter was appointed to Dresden, where he became director of the royal electoral choir – now known as the Dresden Staatskapelle – which he had founded back in Torgau. In 1554, he returned to Torgau and lived there until his death in 1570.

The "Grammar School" had been housed by the former monastery buildings since 1557, until eventually, a new building at the promenade was finished in 1835. The monastery buildings were then partially deconstructed or served other purposes, as described above. At Easter 1923, the secondary school moved back to Schlossstraße, because the buildings at the promenade had become too small for the institution, which had meanwhile been renamed after Field Marshal General August von Mackensen. After World War II, classes at the Torgau secondary school were already resumed on 8th June 1945. From the building of the Wall until the German reunification, the school was called Extended Secondary School "Ernst Schneller". Since the 1980s, it annually recorded about 100 students in both year 11 and 12.

In summer 1990, about 120 students of year 9 and 10 started school at the "Gymnasium", followed by another 120 of year 7 in 1991. With an eye toward the implementation of the eight-year higher secondary education system in summer 1992, the council of the administrative district of Torgau decided to set up a school with four parallel classes at Schlossstraße and to acquire the abbey, which was property of the town. The council also looked after the prompt planning and realisation of the building project. The first stone was laid in 1994, and on 8th December 1995, the new and annex building could already be handed over. And finally, exactly two years later on 8th December 1997, the new school hall was finished. At the inauguration of the new building, the school was named "Johann-Walter-Gymnasium Torgau".

At the moment, about 700 students from year 5 to 12 are being prepared for their examinations of the higher education entrance qualification, the Abitur. The more than 600 years of school history have brought forth so many teachers who would deserve to be named and honoured in this article. However, these two must be mentioned: Iceland researcher Professor Dr Paul Herrmann and artist Gustav Hagemann.

Apart from maintaining the musical and artistic traditions, the school meets all the requirements for the imparting of modern higher level secondary education, promotes language, sporting and scientific skills and teaches young people to act responsibly. ●

The renovated abbey, which now serves as school hall, and houses concerts, exhibitions, conferences, and also examinations

The school did not only have important teachers, but also students who would later help control the country's fate, like Egon Bahr, the creator of the "Ostpolitik" under Willy Brandt, and the German Federal Minister of Education Johanna Wanka.

▶ **DR HELMUT GRAUL**
was principle of the Johann-Walter-Gymnasium from 1990 to 2010.

CHVR-FVRSTL: SÄCHS:
STADT v. AMBT
TORGAW
Das Rath haus
Die Kloster Kirche
St. Nicolai Kirch
AMBT DÜBEN
AMBT EULENBURG
WURTZEN
PRETZSCH
AMBT OSCHAT

Torgau – the Saxon Town

From Saxony to Prussia and back again. A short journey through more than one thousand years of history

BY HANSJOCHEN HANCKE

The town with currently only about 20,000 inhabitants celebrated its one thousandth birthday a long time ago. Torgau was already mentioned in a document of Emperor Otto II in 973. The popular crossing of the river Elbe guaranteed a swift development of the later castle and merchants' settlement. Torgau's rise was especially promoted by the attainment of the electoral dignity by the Wettins in 1423. At the end of the 15th century, the castle and town occupied an important role within the Wettin system of government. The Elbe flow line from Wittenberg via Torgau and Meissen to Dresden was "the political-strategic backbone of Wettin power" (Karlheinz Blaschke). In 1979, the town became a heritage area. It is considered to be the best maintained Renaissance town in Germany.

The Elbe gate of Hartenfels Castle leads to the entrance of the Bottle Tower

Subsequently to the Partition of Leipzig between the brothers Elector Ernest and Duke Albert in 1485, Torgau passed to the Ernestine line of electors. The flourish of art under Elector Frederick the Wise and the great dynastic festivities of the Wettins strengthened the town's economic situation. With Elector John the Steadfast's accession to power in 1525, and under his son and successor John Frederick the Magnanimous, Torgau became the most important residence and "capital" of the Electorate of Saxony. The pictures of Torgau by Lucas Cranach the Elder document this great time of prosperity in the second quarter of the 16th century.

Wittenberg was the intellectual and Torgau the political centre of the Lutheran Reformation. And it is exactly this political aspect that is being described a little sentimentally since the 19th century, when Torgau is referred to as the "nursemaid of the Reformation". Torgau's solitary status in Reformation times was defined by its function as electoral residence and the consequent political events.

The Ernestine Electors had granted protection to Luther and the early Reformation. In this secure environment, the new theology could develop even without initial institutional support. Frederick the Wise's motto from 1522 V D M I AE ("verbum domini manet in aeternum": The Word of the Lord Endures Forever) finally became the motto of the Reformation itself. The setup of an Evangelical national church during the apparently calm years from 1526 onwards would become a model case. The "Articles of Torgau" as the foundation of the Augsburg Confession and the turnaround of Torgau in 1530 regarding the crucial question of the right to resist the Emperor were cornerstones.

The language of the Electoral Saxon Chancellery, which had been situated in Torgau since 1485, doubtlessly had an impact on the development of the unified German language, as it had a more than just normative impact on Luther's Bible translation.

The earliest Reformation monument may be the dedication board of 1545 in the Castle Chapel in Torgau. For the Reformation, the castle wing housing the Castle Chapel, the Elector's

"Torgau has always been my delight ..."

ELECTOR JOHN FREDERICK THE MAGNANIMOUS

Dedication board, made in 1545 by Oswalt Hilger from Freiberg on the occasion of the construction of the Castle Chapel, with medallions picturing Luther, Elector John Frederick and his sons

private rooms and the "beautiful oriel", which is the architectonic masterpiece aside from the Great Stair Turret, generally is the most important one. This part of the castle containing the chapel consecrated by Luther, the Electors' private rooms and the Bottle Tower is the only utilisation unit of the castle's Early Renaissance buildings that can be reconstructed. Here, the only possible way of permanent utilisation is to feature a Reformation-based exhibition. In 2003, the "Initiativkreis Schloss Hartenfels" (Hartenfels Castle initiative) presented a position paper containing all facts and respective ideas concerning this exhibition. On this basis, the castle's inclusion in the UNESCO World Heritage is being discussed at the moment.

In the years between 1505 and 1551, the population doubled from about 3,000 to nearly 6,000 people. This time generally was a great leap forward in development. The town was more important, and also bigger than Dresden, and was approximating Leipzig in terms of population. The events of the Reformation resonated with the citizens and thus, the new theology was already taken on in 1523. This prosperity would continue until 1631. However, Saxony's entry into the Thirty Years' War on the side of Sweden, and the following volte-face changed things completely. In 1637, the Swedish army under Field Marshal Banér, now the enemy, occupied Torgau for about half a year. After that, the town's prosperity was destroyed, and subsequently to the spread of epidemics, the population shrank from more than 6,000 to nearly 2,000 people, among them many orphans.

So the time of grace was ended at half time of the Thirty Years' War. The at least partially developed fortress was consistently fiercely embattled. The bridge over the river Elbe was destroyed, the further environment became desolate, partially by barbarism; approximately half of the houses in Torgau were either destroyed or abandoned. From 1485 until the end of the great religious war in 1648, Torgau was an epicentre of Saxon history under changing conditions, with impacts temporarily even reaching far beyond. But after that time, the motto was: The fortress is fate, with consequences even for present times!

The strategically convenient location at one of the most important Elbe crossings in Saxony still bestowed the town with special attention at later acts of war. Especially the Seven Years' War (1756–1763) had disastrous impacts. Torgau was precisely not just an important Elbe crossing, "but the key position for the control of the Elbe water way to Bohemia and of the plateau ranging from here via Meissen to Freiberg" (Rudolf Mielsch). In the course of the war, the town constantly changed hands, especially from 1759 onwards. In autumn 1760, the war-political and overall situation forced King Frederick II to seek the decisive battle: The Prussians pre-

Panorama of Torgau with the fortifications in the foreground, at the beginning of the 20th century

As a consequence of the Congress of Vienna in 1815, Torgau passed to Prussia. 175 years later, the overwhelming majority of the citizens of the district voted for the return to the Saxon federation.

View of the earthenware manufactory "Villeroy & Boch" from the journal "Keramos" from 1941

vailed on 3rd November 1760 in the most modern battle of the 18th century, which probably also caused the most victims at its time. By the end of the war, the town was economically ruined due to the long duration of quartering. The desolate castle became a workhouse. The following four decades of peace until the beginning of the Napoleonic Wars were not sufficient for the economic recovery after the impoverishment, which was reported throughout Saxony.

In 1806, Saxony is forced by Napoleon to enter into the Confederation of the Rhine, but it is also granted kingdom status. After the slighting of Dresden, Torgau is chosen to become its substitute fortress. On 29th November 1810, the Royal Decree on the construction of the Saxon and Elbe Fortress in Torgau was enacted. Once again the Napoleonic Wars put a strain on the strategic town in the most dreadful way. By resolution of the Congress of Vienna in 1815, Saxony lost nearly two thirds of its territory to Prussia and was approximately reduced to the former Albertine area: Torgau becomes Prussian!

The Saxon fortress experiences an advantageous development as Prussian Elbe fortress by the Kingdom of Prussia. (▸ p. 24) However, not a single shot was fired by the new fortress at the Saxon border until its slighting in 1889. The close link to a strong garrison – at the beginning of the 20th century, three regiments were mainly based in Torgau – brought wealth and conciliation with Prussia. The garrison became the all in all service-oriented town's economic basis.

The cultural life, including the cultivation of music, could compete with much larger cities. So it was affectionately called "Little Potsdam".

Although the boundaries set by the cordon of fortresses had protected the historic town centre throughout the entire 19th century, it also prevented industrialisation. For the mere connection to the existing railway network in 1872, strong doubts concerning the routing through a fortress had to be cleared up and expensive technical solutions to be found. The town had been excluded from the wide transportation system. The opening of the town and planning of a more independent development that had become possible with the town's slighting lead to the urban development plan of 1895, according to which the fortress ground plan was maintained and new residential areas as well as industrial sites were designated. On this base, there have hardly been any blunders in recent decades.

After the end of World War I, there was an increased quest for attracting industries. In 1926, the glass factory and "Villeroy & Boch" were set up – soon followed by Europe's most modern earthenware manufactory with 1,200 employees in 1939. At the end of World War II, this establishment became subject to reparation in the truest sense of the word, which enforced a new beginning. But it was already restituted as fayance manufactory at the beginning of October 1990. During the further industrial development, the glass factory, having evolved into the GDR's largest manufacturer of flat glass in the post-war decades, stood out. Today it belongs to the important French corporation "St. Gobain".

Towards the end of World War II, Torgau gets into international limelight. In commemoration of this, the festival-like ELBE DAY® is celebrated every year. The message of the meeting of American and Soviet troops on 25th April 1945 inspired even the beginning of the collaboration of the new League of Nations, and led to the world-famous arranged photo of 26th April.

The town, which was at first solely occupied by American forces, experienced the not-agreed crossing of the river Elbe by the Red Army on 3rd May 1945, whereon the Americans pulled back to the river Schwarzer Graben, where they set up checkpoints and used the villa of a businessman as commandant's office. And so this first meeting point temporarily became Germany's first parted town – almost an omen for the future division of Europe.

The establishment of the Soviet occupation zone in Germany caused a change in all elements of economic and social life, and Torgau was no exception: It experienced the repeal of the regional court and almost all important institutions, the winding-up of all associations, land reform and all sorts of measures against businesses and members of the bourgeois and educated classes – up until the mid-fifties. In addition to that, "integrative" provisions in the agricultural sector caused a population decline with indications of depopulation. Eventually, in the light of the establishment of the flat glass combine, thousands of new inhabitants were attracted to the town at the end of the 1960s.

In the national referendum of 1990, the citizens of the district of Torgau voted in favour of Saxony and thereby, after 175 years, corrected the dynastic decision of the Congress of Vienna which had forcibly separated the area of Torgau from Saxony. Torgau's location directly on the banks of the river Elbe, a German stream of fate, represents the age of Lutheran Reformation and the Ernestine Electors connected to it, but also the overall incredible destruction that took place in the "Swedish Year" of 1637 and in the French fortress in 1813. However, the townscape characterised by the castle and bourgeois houses of the 16th/17th century was important and, therefore, solid enough to endure over time. ●

▶ **DR HANSJOCHEN HANCKE**
is a former executive library director.

Background image: Hans Sigismund Ulrici, "Churfürstl. Sächs. Stadt v. Ambt Torgav ..." (Saxon Town of Amt Torgau), around 1710/20. [Hauptstaatsarchiv Dresden, 12884 Karten und Risse, Schr. 14, F. 4 Nr. 8 (MF 4996)]

ELBE DAY®

On 25th April 1945, soldiers of the Soviet Army's 58th Guards Rifle Division and the US Army's 69th Infantry Division experienced a history-charged encounter at the river Elbe near Torgau. American and Soviet patrols had already coincidently met shortly before near Strehla. The meeting of the Allied forces visualised the merging of the eastern and western fronts and announced the close end of World War II. On the destroyed Elbe bridge, Lt William Robertson and Lt Alexander Sylvashko joined hands. To spread the symbolic character of the meeting worldwide, the formal handshake was repeated the next day and the picture of it sent to all major news agencies.

Today it is contained in nearly every school- and history-book of the world. In commemoration of this historic event, Torgau celebrates the ELBE DAY® every year at the end of April.

▶ www.elbeday.de

STADT TORGAU
Schloß Hartenfels
Schloß Hartenfels inwendig
Wappen
Der Grafschaft Torgau Der Stadt Torgau
Dommitzsch
Belgern
Schilda
AMBT LIBENWERDE

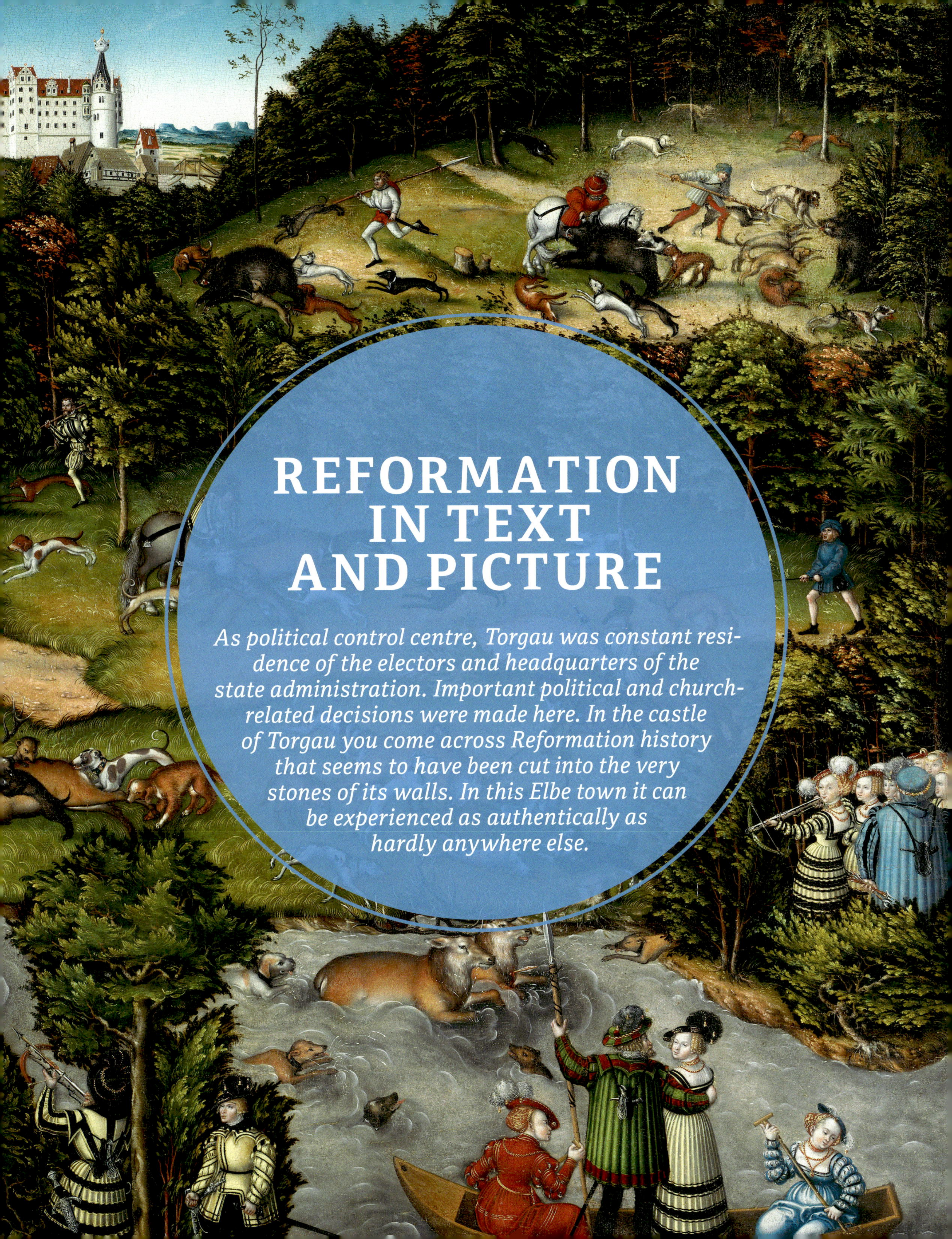

REFORMATION IN TEXT AND PICTURE

As political control centre, Torgau was constant residence of the electors and headquarters of the state administration. Important political and church-related decisions were made here. In the castle of Torgau you come across Reformation history that seems to have been cut into the very stones of its walls. In this Elbe town it can be experienced as authentically as hardly anywhere else.

Torgau – Electoral Residence

The political control centre during the Reformation period

BY ARMIN KOHNLE

Subsequently to the victory at the battle of Mühlberg on 24th April 1547, Emperor Charles V enfeoffed Maurice, Duke of Saxony (1521–1553) with the Electorate of Saxony. He would later lay the foundations for the Religious Peace of Augsburg with the Treaty of Passau

The German territories of the 16th century did not have capitals as we have them today. However, those medieval times when kings and princes ruled their countries out of the saddle were over at about 1500. The modern bureaucratic state began to emerge. Linked to this was the development of more permanent places of government. Since the lands of the Wettins had been divided into an Ernestine Electorate and an Albertine Duchy in 1485, the Albertines used Dresden, and the Ernestines used Torgau, Wittenberg, Lochau (now Annaburg) and Weimar as such governmental places. Among the Ernestine residences, Torgau was the most important, even more important than Wittenberg with its university, founded in 1502, at which Martin Luther worked. While the Ernestine rulers were only infrequent and hardly ever permanent guests of the intellectual and sacral (All Saints Seminary) centre at Wittenberg, the political control centre at Torgau was the constant residence of the Electors and their court, as well as the headquarters of the state administration.

In the years between the Treaty of Leipzig of 1485 and the disastrous defeat of the Ernestines in the Schmalkaldic War in 1547, the town was prestigiously geared to the needs of the court. The Electors Frederick the Wise (1463, Elector 1486–1525) and John Frederick (1503, Elector 1532–1547) were both born in Torgau. Especially John (1468, Elector 1525–1532) and John Frederick gave Torgau a capital-like status in the Ernestine Electorate. Consequently, the town had its heyday in their years. However, with the defeat of 1547 and the following rise of Dresden as capital residence of Albertine Saxony, to which Torgau belonged now, this time of prosperity came to a sudden end.

But during Martin Luther's lifetime, Torgau was the place where the political course for the Reformation in Electoral Saxony and in the whole Empire was made on numerous occasions. Accordingly, Luther often came to the town: There is proof of no less than 41 visits. Luther maintained various relations to churchmen and teachers in Torgau. The preacher and superintendent Gabriel Zwilling (▶ p. 52), the Latinist and principal Marcus Crodel and the cantor Johann Walter (▶ p. 48) were all part and parcel of his network. But principally, Luther's Torgau contacts were consistently entangled with the religious policy of the Ernestine Electors, especially after Elector John had succeeded his brother Frederick in 1525. Unlike Frederick the Wise, who had protected Luther and sympathised with the reformatory theology but had never openly promoted the Reformation, John was a true Protestant ruler, who took it as his mission to establish the Wittenberg theology in the country and to defend the Reformation against its enemies.

In the first half of the 16th century, Torgau was not only the political centre of the Ernestine Electors, but also the place where the Augsburg Confession was prepared and the alliance for the defence of the Reformation was forged.

Torgau repeatedly played an important role on the long road leading to the formation of the Schmalkaldic League, in which the larger part of the Protestant imperial estates congregated. In the run-up to the Diet of Speyer in 1526, Electoral Saxony and Hesse allied in Gotha against a possible attack. The treaty of alliance was drafted in Torgau on 2nd Mai 1526, which is why this first attempt to establish a Protestant military alliance is referred to as League of Torgau and Gotha. Although an effective league of Protestant estates could not be achieved at that time, it was the first occasion on which the two leading powers of the Protestant imperial estates, Electoral Saxony and Hesse, came to the fore. The formation of a military alliance to defend the word of God was not only a politically charged issue, but also a theological one. Martin Luther and the Wittenberg reformers repeatedly commented on the topic of the legitimacy of such an alliance.

This raised the question about the right to resist the Emperor. Luther consistently stated that armed resistance to the God-given authority would mean resistance to God's order itself, thus hindering substantially the attempts of the late 1520s to achieve a Protestant military alliance. Luther viewed the Emperor – at that time Habsburg Charles V – as an authority appointed by God, directly drawing on the conditions described in the New Testament. As instructed by St. Paul in his Epistle to the Romans (13:1–7), everyone owed obedience to the Emperor. Just as the mayor of Torgau owed obedience to the Elector of Saxony, Luther once said, the Elector of Saxony owed obedience to the Emperor. With that, there were no grounds for a military alliance for the protection of the gospel.

However, developments culminated in 1530, when Emperor Charles V held an Imperial Diet again, after nearly a decade had passed. From the Emperor's invitation it was to be understood that the Protestant estates would be granted the opportunity to account for their religion. The Wittenberg reformers – Luther as well as Philipp Melanchthon, Justus Jonas and Johannes Bugenhagen – met at the Old Superintendenture in March 1530 to consult on a Protestant Confession that could be presented to the Emperor. The result were the Articles of Torgau that would become the basis for the Confession of Augsburg drafted by Melanchthon at the Imperial Diet. This Confession of Augsburg, which was presented to the Emperor by John, Elector of Saxony, and Philip, Landgrave of Hesse, in union with other Protestant estates and towns, still is the primary confession of the Lutheran Church today.

◄ P. 36/37
Lucas Cranach the Elder, "Hofjagd auf Hirsche und Bären", 1540 ("Hunting near Hartenfels Castle", © The Cleveland Museum of Art, John L. Severance Fund: 1958.425)

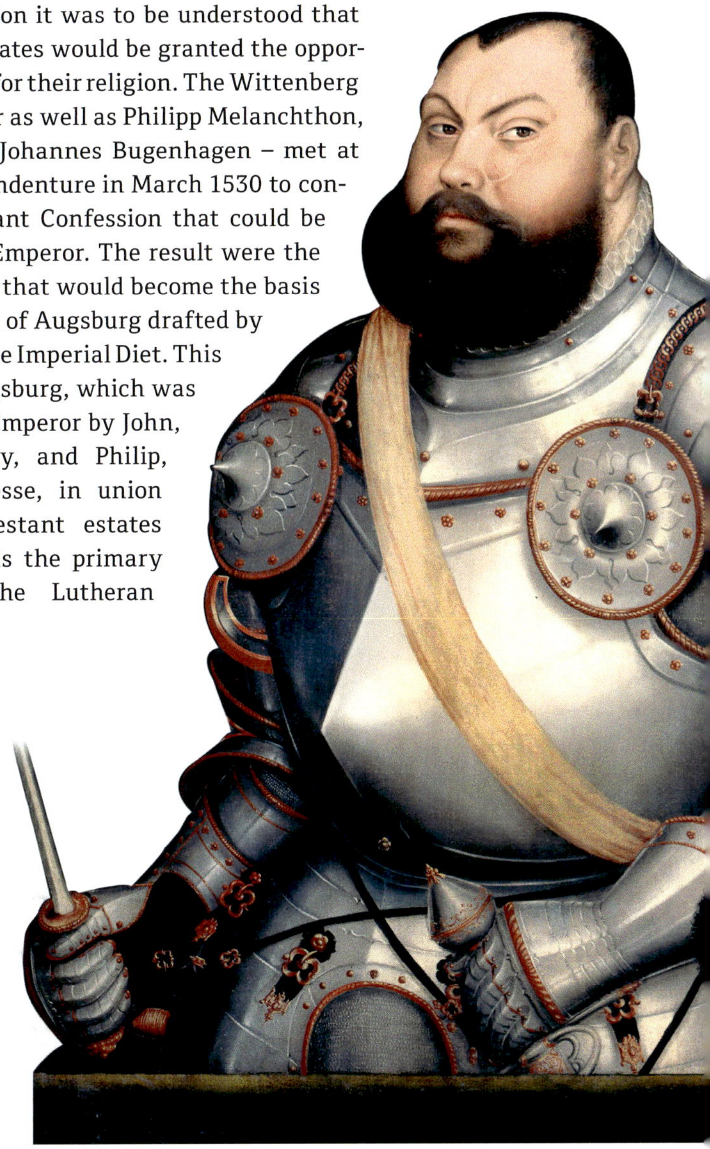

Subsequently to the Capitulation of Wittenberg of 19th May 1547, Elector John Frederick I, the Magnanimous (1503–1554), lost his title and a great part of his territory to his cousin Duke Maurice

Elector Frederick III, the Wise (1463–1525), painting adapted from Lucas Cranach the Elder (workshop)

▶ Elector John the Steadfast, (1468–1532), painting adapted from Lucas Cranach the Elder (workshop)

▶ P. 41
The "Great Gate", main entrance of Hartenfels Castle since 1623, with the electoral coat of arms from the time of John George I

After the Emperor had rejected this confession and the Diet of Augsburg had ended in open conflict, the formation of a military alliance was on the table again. First of all, the theological reservations had to be eliminated. The crucial discussion between Electoral Saxon lawyers and politicians and Luther took place in October 1530 in Torgau. The Reformer was made aware that the Elector of Saxony's relation to the Emperor could by no means be equalised with that of the Roman Emperors to their office holders. The Elector of Saxony was an authority in his own right, and not just subject to the Emperor. Luther had to accept this instruction and declared the formation of a military alliance a secular issue which he would no longer comment on as a theologian. This "Turnaround of Torgau" paved the way for the formation of the Schmalkaldic League around the end of 1530.

The visits Luther paid to Torgau in 1530 were doubtlessly the most successful ones for the further progress of the Reformation. But he also travelled the 50 kilometres from Wittenberg to Torgau on ceremonial occasions. In 1536 he attended the wedding of Philip I, Duke of Pomerania, and Mary of Saxony, the oldest daughter of Elector John. Hartenfels Castle was already a splendid location for such events at that time. However, it was embellished in Renaissance style during Luther's lifetime. In 1544 Luther was the first one to preach at the Torgau Castle Chapel, thus consecrating the first Protestant church construction. This preach is often quoted, because Luther defined in it what should happen in a Protestant place of worship: "that our dear Lord himself may speak to us through his holy word and we respond to him through prayer and praise." For his numerous services Luther was often remunerated with food donations from the Torgau food provisions – beer, wine or cider, fish, corn or chickens. ●

▶ **PROFESSOR DR ARMIN KOHNLE**
holds the chair for Late Middle Ages, Reformation and Territorial Ecclesiastical History at the Faculty of Theology at Leipzig University.

The Reformation in Torgau

The Torgau Council in between the Elector and the people – "in these fast, dangerous times and events"

BY JÜRGEN HERZOG

The Monastery Tower in 1525, history painting from the first half of the 19th century

This is the character of the time at the beginning of the 16th century: The arising Reformation movement faced a deep, late medieval piety. At the same time, the abuses by the Roman Catholic Church led to hardly bearable excesses.

In the Electorate of Saxony, peace and considerable wealth dominated the long reign of Frederick the Wise. He was a Roman Catholic himself, but protected the reformers around Martin Luther and let them accomplish their mission. The parish church of Torgau with its 16 altars had become the court chapel. There was a cloister between the castle and the Elector's galleries in the church. In 1493, Elector Frederick had donated the pilgrimage church "Zum Heiligen Kreuz" (of the Holy Cross) along with a Saint Sepulchre. This church, which was also called "The Beauty", was located directly in front of the hospital gate and was very popular.

In terms of piety, the Torgau Council and citizens were in no way inferior to the Elector. The common church was the Nikolaikirche on the market square with its eight altars. Nine brotherhoods, which were mainly financed by the local craftsmen, had their altars here. But there also was a council brotherhood, which had been affiliated to the Franciscan Brotherhood in 1497.

The number of private masses held for the salvation of the souls of decedents and their benefactors increased conspicuously. Some priests were appointed specifically for this purpose. The most costly mourning ceremony was the one held for Duchess Sophie, who had died in 1503. It had to be arranged with singing and preaching by 24 priests, the cantor, the schoolmaster with all his pupils and five paupers, mourning at her grave.

The criticism that arose in the early times of the Reformation soon fell on fertile soil among the citizens. The preacher Valentin Tham spoke out against indulgence as early as 1518. From 1519 onwards, baptisms were held in German. Surely Martin Luther also held his first mass in Torgau in 1519 in this church. When the Bishop of Meissen questioned the preacher here in 1522 to *move in on the destruction of the order of the Holy Christian Church*, there was no identifiable result.

First of all, the new theology represented by Martin Luther stated that forgiveness of sins was granted through the mercy of God alone, but not through good deeds, paid-for private masses, indulgence or veneration of relics. The first who were hit by this were the begging monks of the Pauline order of Leipzig and the Augustine order of Herzberg, who came here for alms and night quarters. They were banished from the town in 1521 and 1522. But this threatened poor relief, and new avenues had to be explored. For this purpose, the Council introduced a "Common Box" for collecting donations. It was first mentioned in 1522. Six superintendents were appointed. The hospitals also had to be reorganised. So the next April the Council decided to sell the Katharinenkirche (St. Catherine's church) to the council brotherhood and use the money to build an infirmary. Subsequently, in 1523 the St. Catherine hospital was united with the Holy Spirit hospital and the St. James hospital of the St. James Brotherhood.

The Council was caught in the middle: The Elector's protecting attitude towards the Roman Catholic system opposed the citizens' demand for reforms. The radicalisation in Wittenberg had already required precautionary measures in 1522, when the Council had all guns and other arms fixed for a possible emergency.

In March the citizens were threatened with punishment for eating meat during Lent, but only if the Elector himself would order this punishment. However, those who removed paintings from the churches, burned or otherwise abused them, should be punished as criminals. The Roman Catholic procession "of the figures" should be kept for the moment.

The year of 1523 became a year of trouble and complete change of heart among the citizens. Several young roof tylers and cutlers roamed the lanes

Martin Luther in 1528, painting adapted from Lucas Cranach the Elder (workshop)

at Carnival, carrying a cross and singing vulgar songs. In the end they threw the cross onto the rectory's doorstep.

The former Torgau tax collector Leonhard Köppe made a great stir when he helped nine nuns to flee the convent of Nimbschen on 5th April and another five nuns to flee the convent of Sitzenroda on 22nd May.

The former Augustinian friar Gabriel Zwilling, who was promoted by Martin Luther, became a preacher in Torgau. The Council decided on 17th February 1524 to let him work with the Roman

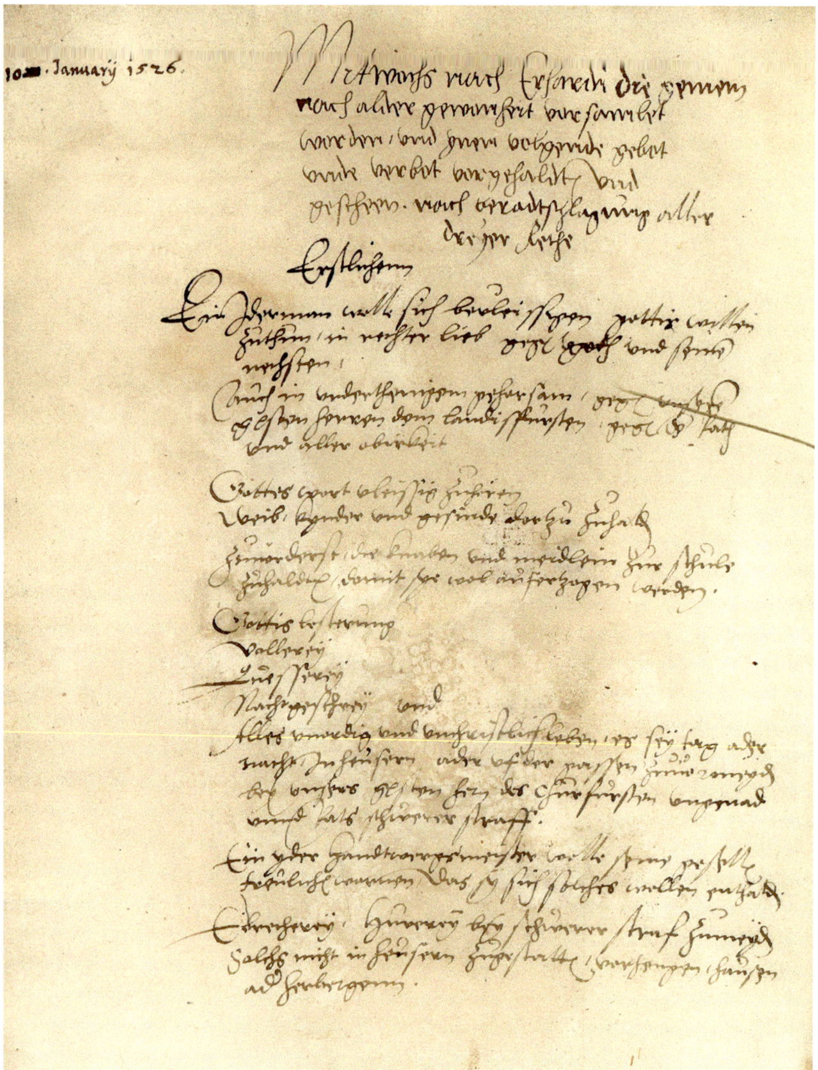

From the Council's records of 10th January 1526 (▶ p. 45), admonition of the citizens to obey

Catholic priest Thomas Moller. Zwilling seems to have lived in the rectory with him.

The Council now had great difficulties to maintain the town's order. The gathering citizens were repeatedly admonished to stop the blasphemy and nightly clamours, pay their dues to the church and priesthood, and to cherish religion. Common theft, for example of curtains and altar cloths from the churches, got out of control. The Council now also warned that the monks and the monastery must not be harmed, according to the Elector's order.

The year of 1525 bore open disputes between the Council, the supporters of the Reformation and the Elector along with the Roman Catholic clergy.

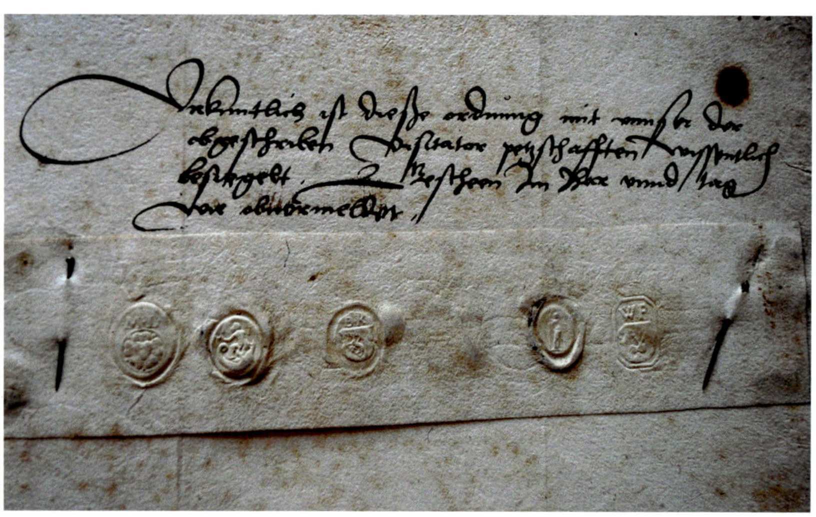

Seal on the Visitor's report of 1529

In the course of the Reformation, the religious brotherhoods began to break up, donations were no longer made to the monasteries, and even the public women's refuge was closed, *as it was against God*.

The eventful year of 1525 became a real test of the relations between Elector Frederick and the Council. Of all people, it were the electoral tailor Günter Braun and the master gunner Paul Resch who led the storming of the Franciscan monastery after the Carnival celebrations in the night from 28th February to 1st March, when 24 citizens and sons of citizens caused great damage and spread terror in the town. The Elector, who had just received a delegation of Archduke Ferdinand, suspected the Council of having plotted the storming, threatened the town with the loss of jurisdiction and demanded compensation for the damage. The fugitive monastery invaders were up for death penalty. However, his brother Duke John judged more mildly, so that only a small, or in fact, no penalty at all was imposed after Frederick the Wise's death on 5th May.

Due to the very insecure circumstances in which the Roman Catholic priest was living now, he saw himself forced to, in the presence of Gabriel Zwilling, pass the St. George hospital to the Council, who immediately sold the church and all buildings. Priest Thomas Moller died on 1st May 1525.

After Elector Frederick's death, the remaining six monks of the Franciscan monastery no longer felt secure, and thus handed their jewels and a house over to the Council on 7th May, seeking protection. Everything was sold to the benefit of the Common Box. At the community's request, Gabriel Zwilling was appointed as pastor at the town meeting of 17th May.

On 20th August 1525, the citizens and the Council revered the new Elector John, who encouraged the reformatory changes. From 30th August onwards, the court resided in Torgau almost uninterruptedly. The Elector claimed the monastery buildings for himself, and the monastic community had to give way. The Reformation movement had finally prevailed in the town.

The year of 1526 was now characterised by common disciplining. On 10th of January the Council demanded:

Every man shall affect to do the will of God in true love for God and his neighbour, and also in subservient obedience to our most gracious Lord the Elector, to the Council and all authorities. [...] Any kind of disorderly and ungodly life, at either day or night, inside houses or in the streets, shall be avoided and subject to our Lord the Elector's disgrace and the Council's stiff punishment.

The girls' school was mentioned for the first time, its establishment certainly being Gabriel Zwilling's achievement. The conclusion of the admonition of the citizens with a prayer was also something new: *God give all this, for his praise and the blessing of our souls, and for lasting peace. Amen.*

When the first church visitation was conducted in Martin Luther's presence in 1529, the reformers came upon almost completely regulated conditions. The parish church was confirmed as sermon church, as were the abbey and the hospital church. The Nikolaikirche, despite being the town's initial early Reformation church, was finally closed. ●

The Spalatin House

Where the reformers were frequent guests

BY JÜRGEN HERZOG

Georg Spalatin's parsonage on one of the town's smallest alleys, the so-called blind alley, presumably was a very busy place. It is still there today, close to the electoral castle: the narrow, gable-topped little house. It is one of Torgau's oldest buildings and was exposed to the rashes of time for many years. In 1493, Elector Frederick the Wise decided to have it built above an even older, deep cellar. Before he, being a deeply religious Christian, set out on a pilgrimage to the cradle of Christianity at faraway Jerusalem, he donated a new altar, the one called "Zum Neuen Kreuz" (of the new cross) at the Torgau parish church, and a pilgrimage chapel outside the hospital gate, called "Zum Heiligen Kreuz" (of the Holy Cross). At the latter he also had a "Saint Sepulchre" built upon his return, following the Jerusalem example. The chapel with byname "The Beauty" has disappeared. What is left is the residence of the pastor, unique in Saxony in terms of completeness.

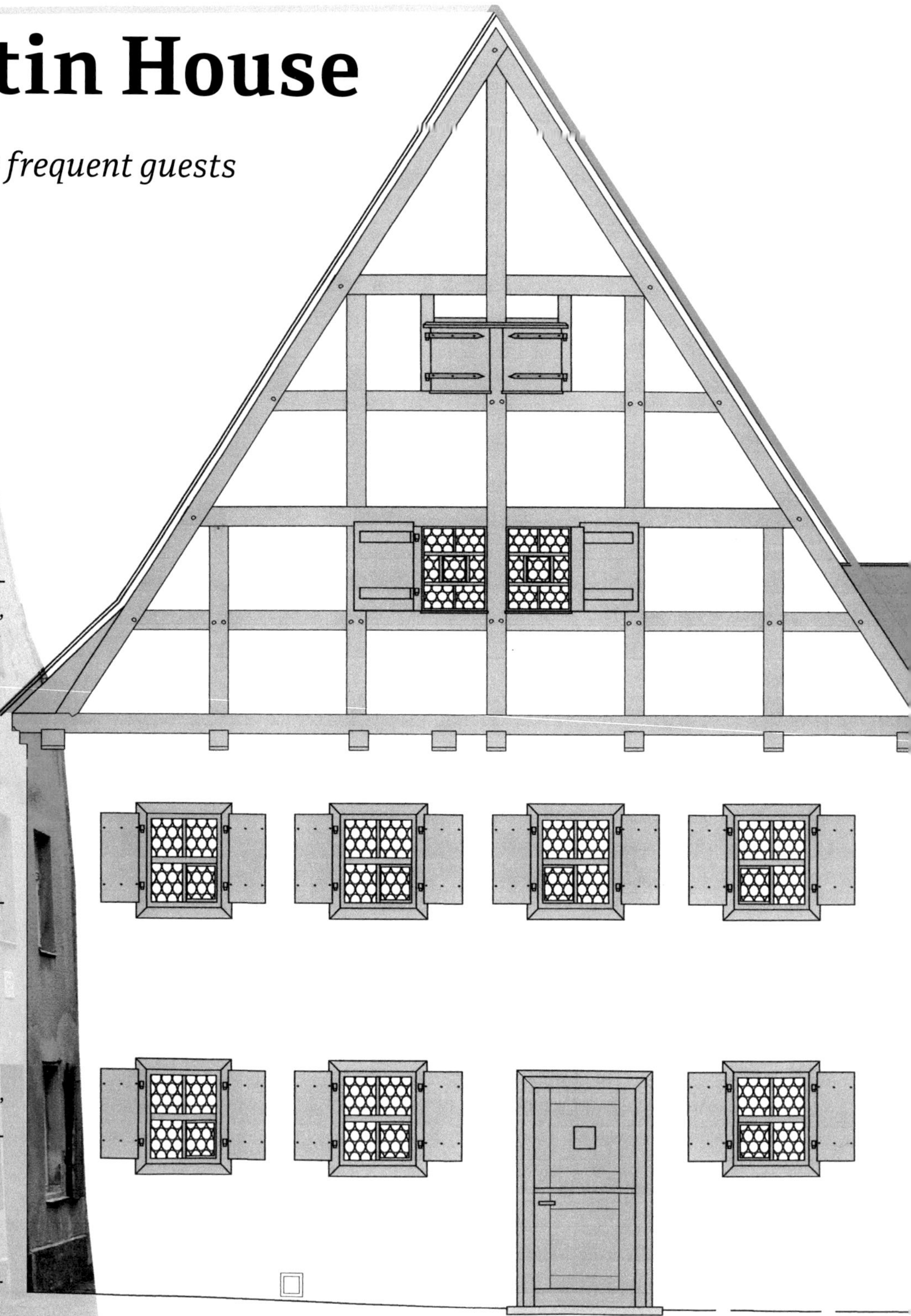

Reconstruction of the facade by architect Antje Hainz, Meissen

Having been freed from all later additions, the pastor's parlour, bedroom and the black walls in the kitchen, the realm of the cook – an employee that every priest needed – can now be recognised. In 1523, the privy secretary and court chaplain of the Elector, Georg Spalatin, was enfeoffed the altar along with the house and fifty guilders a year for alimentation. By this time, Spalatin had renounced the altar service along with daily masses and the Corpus Christy processions a long time ago. As a convinced adherent of Martin Luther's, he had come to dislike these overcome traditions. His benefactor, the Elector, knew that, too. However, with this benefice he

Georg Spalatin, originally Burkhardt (1484–1545)

had achieved his aim of securing a lifelong alimentation for his intimate counsellor. Georg Spalatin now served the Reformation movement more passionately than ever before. Would it have been possible without him at all? Hardly likely, as he acted as mediator between Martin Luther and the particular Electors.

The house was in Spalatin's possession until 1533. The current Elector John Frederick the Magnanimous, whose tutor he had been here in Torgau from 1508 to 1511, permitted him to sell it. But the income was paid nevertheless. This was a special favour, as all other church property was donated to the Common Box, from which the poor, the clergy and the school, but also the church and its associated buildings including the hospital had to be maintained. Today, the small and time-worn house which was inhabited by almost twenty generations after Spalatin is the only one of the scholar's residences that stood the test of time. The committed members of the friends' association for monument preservation took on the task of maintaining it and restoring its appearance of once, when it was inhabited and experienced by the priests, and Spalatin. Upon completion, it will house an exhibition to commemorate Georg Spalatin. A second part of the exhibition will be dedicated to another important Torgau citizen, who had spent almost his entire life in this town: the composer Johann Walter (▶ p. 48). Appreciated by Martin Luther, he committed his whole musical skill to the Reformation. Walter is the father of Protestant church music and of the secular church choir. The school at which he taught now houses the Johann-Walter-Gymnasium (▶ p. 28). He founded the first town choir ever: the Johann Walter Choir of Torgau, which is still active today.

The federal and state governments, the German Foundation for Monument Protection "Deutsche Stiftung Denkmalschutz", the Torgau town government and enthusiastic citizens all work together to restore the Spalatin House and to make the exhibition a reality. ●

An Association Saves Monuments

After decades of vacancy, the poor little house behind the former Bäckerwall (baker's wall) was in danger of falling in or being torn down. But sixteen brave citizens of Torgau and Dresden who were keen of the remaining structure plucked up the courage to incorporate an association to save the building. They chipped in and bought the house in 2006, just in time to prevent its definite end. Another enthusiastic auxiliary, Dr Heinz Murmann, fell in love with the tiny house when he visited Torgau. His donation helped to raise the necessary sum for its planned reconstruction as a monument. In 2010, the little museum at the "Handwerkerhaus" could finally be opened to enhance the Torgau Museum Path.

By now, the friends' association "Förderverein für Denkmalpflege" has optimistically taken on another project: the "Spalatinhaus" on Katharinengasse. This project is sponsored by the Federal Government, the Saxon Government and the German Foundation for Monument Protection "Deutsche Stiftung Denkmalschutz". Meanwhile, the friends' association has twenty members, but more fellows and sponsors are always welcome.

▶ www.museum-torgau.de

The "First Cantor" Johann Walter

Torgau as the cradle of Protestant choir music

BY CHRISTA MARIA RICHTER

Johann Walter: "Das Christlich Kinderlied D. Martini Lutheri, Erhalt vns Herr etc. [...]". Six part books. Wittenberg, 1566, first music page of the tenor part book. The five introductory stanzas "Erhalt uns, Herr, bei deinem Wort" (sustain us, Lord, in your word) by Luther, which are depicted above, were set to music by Walter in his "opus ultimum" (last printed opus) as a song-motet with equal parts and different sounding verses

One of the personalities who had a crucial impact on Torgau's town life during Reformation times was the "first cantor" Johann Walter (1496–1570). Together with Martin Luther, he initiated the reform of the "German Mass" in 1525, to which he made a major contribution, not only by writing music. Some of his songs are still being sung at Protestant services, e.g. *Wach auf, wach auf, du deutsches Land* (1561) or Luther's *Mitten wir im Leben sind* (1524), the melody of which was composed by Walter, also the melodies of *Der Herr ist mein getreuer Hirt* and *Herr, für dein Wort sei hoch gepreist* (1524) as well as *All' Morgen ist ganz frisch und neu* (1541), which all had different words during Walter's lifetime. In addition, there are also lyrics written by Walter which now have different melodies, e.g. *Herzlich tut mich erfreuen* (1552) and *Allein auf Gottes Wort* (1566). Walter already published his own movements in his major work *Eyn geystlich Gesangk Buchleyn* (1524 et seqq.), which had been published even before the Reformation was established (1525) in Electoral Saxony, and was reissued several times. One year later he and Luther worked out the German Mass.

Despite of his musical work, the "first cantor" is regarded as the father of Protestant choir music. Around 1526 he rallied adult citizens of Torgau round himself to rehearse – together with the choir schoolboys – the new Latin-German church music and present it at St. Marien church. With this, a new kind of common evangelical music was born, which quickly spread to other communities and has survived in the choirs of the church congregations until today.

However, Walter's great musical commitment was by no means limited to the early Reformation period, as his whole life was devoted to liturgical singing. So, let's have a look at his life.

Johann Walter was born in 1496 in the Ernestine town of Kahla, inheriting his father's name. The family was also called Blanckenmüller, because the father operated the local wind mill. Due to a visual impairment, the son was adopted and raised by a Kahla relative, whose surname was Walter, too. He went to school in Kahla and Rochlitz and took up his studies at Leipzig University. In 1524/25 he started his career as a singer and composer at the Elector's chapel in Torgau. Unfortunately, Elector Frederick the Wise, who had always been eager to enrich his court with music, died only a short time after in 1525. His brother John the Steadfast put no value to filigree music and disbanded the electoral choir in 1526. In order to continue his musical work, Walter founded the town choir. But he did not receive annual donations from the Elector nor funding from the town's Common Box for the purchase of notebooks until the new Elector John Frederick the Magnanimous granted them to him ten years later. Apart from the establishment of a special school cantorate for teaching music to the pupils (1530), Walter received several donations from the Elector, which allowed him to buy a small house in 1532.

However, Walter's greatest wish – his involvement in the courtly church services – was not fulfilled until much later. The town choir was allowed to participate for the first time in 1542, on the occasion of the Elector's wedding, and his services for the court were only paid for regularly in the form of wages and school allowances after the consecration of the Protestant Castle Chapel in 1544.

Johann Walter made Torgau the cradle of Protestant church music.

But this situation, which was ideal for Walter, regrettably changed when Torgau passed to the Albertines at the end of the Schmalkaldic War. Elector Maurice indeed appointed Walter as conductor of his electoral choir, which had been re-established in 1548, but due to conflicts induced by the Leipzig Interim and the appointment of foreign musicians, Walter would not hold this position very long. Between 1550 and 1552, the choir moved to Dresden after the extensive construction works at Dresden Castle had been finished. In 1554, Walter asked to be pensioned and returned to Torgau as a rich man. Anyway, before he retired he was involved in the consecration of the new Castle Chapel in Dresden, which has been used since 1554.

In the final years of his life, Walter produced many compositions and poems, which he dedicated to his former sovereigns. Just as he had started his career as a composer at the Ernestine court, he passed away as a composer in great thankfulness to the Ernestine Electors. He could look back on 74 years of life rich in music, of which he had spent about 45 years in Torgau. ●

▸ **CHRISTA MARIA RICHTER**
works as a freelance music historian.
www.quellenlese.de

New Beginning and End of Life

How Katharina von Bora, Luther's future wife, was linked to Torgau

BY HANS-CHRISTOPH SENS

Katharina von Bora woke up from deep slumber on Easter morning 1523. She heard bells. A full, harmonious ringing had wakened her. She sat up. Where was she? Oh right, in Torgau. Suddenly it all came back to her mind: the flight from Nimbschen convent in the night before Holy Saturday, the long journey hidden on the covered wagon of merchant Leonhard Köppe from Torgau, the arrival at the town late at night. She had barely been able to make out the church on the other side of the street. In this church the bells were ringing so voluminously now. It was high time to rush to early mass. The men who had brought them to Torgau had told them that in this church service had already been held in the Lutheran style for several years. The nuns were eager to hear this. They would spend Easter in Torgau, then they would travel on to Wittenberg to meet Professor Luther. It was him who encouraged the flight, so surely he would continue to help.

Katharina von Bora, referred to as "die Lutherin" (1499–1552), in 1526, painting adapted from Lucas Cranach the Elder

These may have been 24-year-old Katharina von Bora's thoughts when she came to Torgau at Easter 1523 together with eight other nuns, about to enter into secular life. The bells now ring daily in the towers of Nikolaikirche again, where they already hung back at that time. The Nikolaikirche stood rather unattached, on a small cemetery near Leipziger Straße, west of the market square. Today's Town Hall did not exist then. The Torgau citizen Leonhard Köppe lived in Leipziger Straße, only a few steps away. The Nikolaikirche was a succursal church of the town church St. Marien. The priest there had not yet adopted the Lutheran theology. But at Nikolaikirche, priest Valentin Tham was responsible. According to tradition, he had held the first baptism in German as early as 1519, and he had been preaching in German in the Lutheran way since 1520. He is said to have already turned against the sale of indulgence in 1518. Luther's work "Ein Sermon von Ablass und Gnade" (A Sermon on Indulgences and Grace), probably published in March 1518 and soon reprinted many times, had obviously fallen on fertile soil.

Martin Luther had visited Torgau before during an official journey as vicar general of the order of the Augustinian Eremits in 1516. Eventually, he preached in Torgau for the first time in 1519, as is documented by a respective bill of the Council. When Luther passed through Torgau again in 1522 on his journey to Herzberg, he was hailed for his steadfastness before the Emperor and his Empire. Again, a bill of the council documents that 38 Groschen were spent on food for himself, his companions and six horses, and that a barrel of beer was brought to Wittenberg for him for one Schock and nine Groschen. During these early visits, Martin Luther must have met the merchant Leonhard Köppe, who was a former council member and tax collector in Torgau. Despite the fact that Köppe was nearly 20 years older than

Epitaph of Katharina Luther, d. 20th December 1552, in St. Marien town church

Luther, the two became friends. The former council member maintained business relations with Nimbschen convent, and probably became a supporter of Luther's early on. In 1523, Luther entrusted this man with the delicate mission of getting those nuns out of Nimbschen convent who did no longer want to stay there. On 9th April 1523, the Thursday after Easter, Luther wrote an open letter in Wittenberg *to the cautious and wise Leonhard Koppen, citizen of Torgau, my special friend ...*, in which he made public and justified the liberation of the nuns from the Cistercian convent in Nimbschen.

The flight, or liberation, of the nuns from Nimbschen convent was a consequence of Luther's perception of enforced vows as being void and against God's will. Luther praised the flight as the beginning of a new life, equal to the resurrection of Christ from the power of death.

Torgau was Katharina von Bora's first stop on her way into this new life. However, it was only a very short one of two days at the longest. The nuns travelled on to Wittenberg immediately after Easter, where they arrived together with their liberators on Easter Tuesday.

Whether Katharina ever returned to Torgau during her husband's lifetime is not known, although it is conceivable, as Luther often had business here. But there is only proof of her journey to Torgau in September 1552, six and a half years after her husband's death, from which she should never return. Together with her children, Katharina had followed the University of Wittenberg, which had resettled in the buildings of the former Franciscan monastery in Torgau because of a plague epidemic. She was hosted by another widow at the "Haus auf dem Scharfenberge" (House on the Scharfenberge) on today's Katharinengasse. Apparently she fell off the carriage and never recovered from her severe injuries. Katharina Luther, née von Bora, died on 20th December 1552 in Torgau. She was buried only one day later in St. Marien town church. The entire university accompanied her coffin in the funeral procession. Philipp Melanchthon said in a text on Katharina's funeral: *Throughout the entire time of her sickness she consoled and uplifted herself with the Word of God, and eagerly prayed for a peaceful passing away from this life full of grief, and often commended the church and her children to God, begging that the pure theology which the Lord had given back to this last era through her husband's voice may be passed on undistortedly to the generations to come.*

Her children had a gravestone made for her, which can still be seen at St. Marien town church today. The epitaph reads: *ANNO 1552, on 20th DECEMBER Dr Martin Luther's blessed bereaved widow Katharina has passed away peacefully to God here in Torgau.* The exact position of her grave in the town church is not known. ●

▸ **HANS-CHRISTOPH SENS**
is ret. chief consistorial councillor of the Protestant Church in the former church province of Saxony.

Katharina Luther Parlour

In 1523, Torgau was young Katharina von Bora's first stop after her flight from Nimbschen convent on her way into a secular life, and her journey through life as Martin Luther's widow should also end here. She died in this house in 1552 following an accident just outside Torgau's gates. Katharina became a confident woman at Martin Luther's side, who was closely linked to the reformatory work of her husband. In Torgau, the political centre of the Reformation, the Luther family's life often collided with the lives of important citizens of the town. The exhibition containing contemporary graphic works, texts, objects of daily life and artwork connected with Luther's "Mr. Käthe" is dedicated to this extraordinary woman.

▸ www.museum-torgau.de

Gabriel Zwilling – Torgau's First Superintendent

A strong advocate of Reformation matters

BY MARTIN TREU

He was small, plain and one-eyed, but loud. Gabriel Zwilling, who changed his surname to the Greek "Didymus", according to humanist tradition. His year of birth is unknown, although it seems that he was several years younger than Luther. The Augustinian Eremite enrolled at the University of Wittenberg in 1512. After his graduation as Baccalaureus, Luther sent him to the Augustinian monastery of Erfurt in 1517 to study Greek. In 1519, he returned to Wittenberg and graduated as Magister.

However, the talented preacher did not come into public view, until 1521, when Luther resided at the Wartburg. His sermons at the monastery became more and more radical, probably under the influence of Andreas Bodenstein from Karlstadt. Contemporaries admiringly called him a "second Martinus". On 10th January, he led the first iconoclasm of the Reformation. The equipment of the Augustinian chapel, altars, crucifixes and banners were burnt in the monastery's courtyard, and statues were decapitated. Luther's return ended the chaos. Unlike Karlstadt, Zwilling accepted Luther as his leader once more. From now on Luther would regard him as a special friend.

Since Zwilling's appointment as Protestant pastor of Altenburg was not enforceable due to the opposition of the town's Roman Catholic chapter, he became the assistant of the priest of Torgau at the beginning of 1523. According to documents, he had been preaching in the town from 13th December of the same year onwards. He married Elisabeth, the widow of the electoral secretary Hieronymus Rudlauf, on 1st October 1524. It seems that Luther approved of this marriage very much, as the Reformer acted as godfather of Zwilling's first born son in 1526.

On 17th May 1525, the citizens of Torgau unanimously elected him as town pastor, and in 1529 he became superintendent and therefore supervisor of all clergymen in Torgau and its environs. He was appreciated everywhere as a talented preacher. Given the acoustics of contemporary churches, one can assume that the small person possessed a sustaining and clear voice. There is no proof for any connection between Zwilling and the storming of the Torgau Franciscan monastery of 1st March 1525, and it is very unlikely that he was involved. However, his dedicated preaches certainly contributed to the atmosphere that allowed for the attack in the first place.

Usually, a residence house was provided for the current cleric of a parish. And in Torgau Zwilling seems to have lived in such at first. But in addition to it, Luther thought that the Torgau municipality had to make sure that Zwilling and his growing family got their own house. The Council was of different opinion. Instead of donating an available house to him, he was offered to buy one on Rittergasse for 200 guilders. Of course, Zwilling did not have so much money. Now the Elector came to

Entrance of the former Superintendenture at No. 2, Wintergrüne, where Gabriel Zwilling lived and conducted his official duties from 1525 onwards

Luther called the Torgau citizens "rude frogs", who liked to hear the Good News but did not want to provide for an appropriate livelihood of its annunciators.

his aid. However, the building must have been in a very bad condition, as Zwilling appealed to the Elector again in a letter in 1540, asking for further financial benefits for the renovations. This letter is now kept at the Luther House in Wittenberg. Luther already understood in 1535 that the "rude frogs of Torgau" wanted to hear the gospel, but were not ready to appropriately provide for their preacher. But from the town's point of view, it was rather about making the cleric an ordinary citizen, who is not different from anybody else.

After Luther's death and the defeat of the Protestants in the Schmalkaldic War, the new Elector Maurice of Saxony tried to ensure the survival of the Lutheran Church by making some concessions regarding the ceremonies during religious service to the Roman Catholic side at the so-called Leipzig Interim. Zwilling refused to accept the alterations without compromise, even though the Elector himself negotiated with him. He was thus degraded in 1549 and put under arrest in Wittenberg for a short time. However, the old friend of Luther's had many advocates, and eventually was allowed to live in Torgau as a private citizen until he died in 1558. He even received a pension from the Elector, for whose mother he worked as a private preacher at the Torgau castle. ●

▸ **DR MARTIN TREU**
is a theologian and church historian and also works as voluntary CEO for the Luther-Gesellschaft (Luther Association) in Wittenberg.

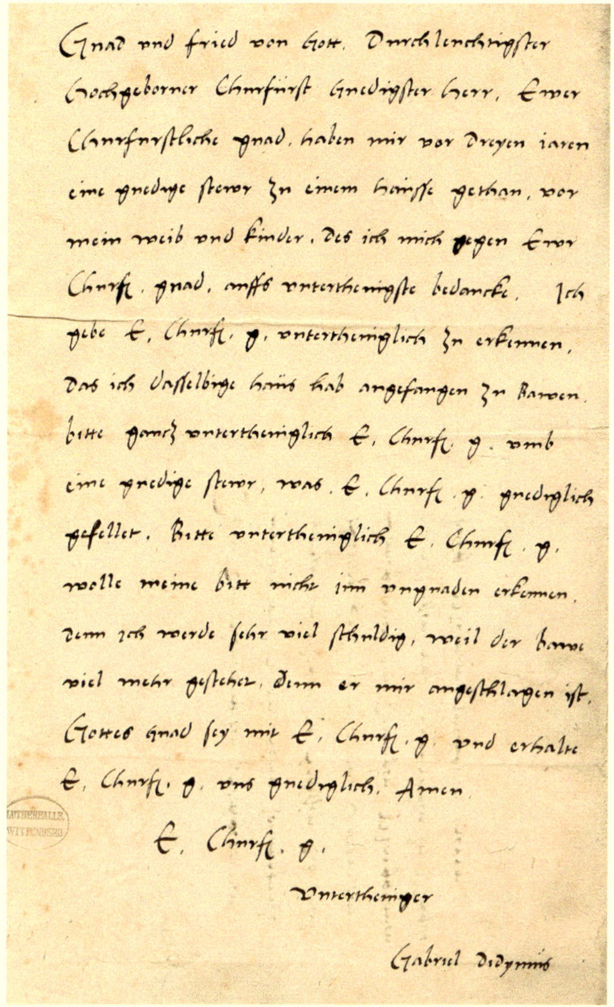

Gnad vnd fried von Gott. Durchleuchtigster
Hochgeborner Churfurst Gnedigster Herr, Ewer
Churfurstliche gnad, haben mir vor dreyen iaren
eine gnedige steuer zu einem hauße gethan, vor
mein weib vnd kinder. Des ich mich gegen Ewer
Churf. gnad, auffs vnterthenigste bedancke. Ich
gebe E. Churf. g. vnterthenigklich zu erkennen,
Das ich dasselbige haus hab angefangen zu bawen.
bitte gantz vnterthenigklich E. Churf. g. vmb
eine gnedige steuer, was E. Churf. g. gnediglich
gefellet. Bitte vnterthenigklich E. Churf. g.
wolle meine bitt nicht im vngnaden erkennen.
Denn ich werde sehr viel schuldig, weil der bawe
viel mehr gestehet, denn er mir angeschlagen ist.
Gottes gnad sey mit E. Churf. g. vnd erhalte
E. Churf. g. vns gnediglich. Amen.

E. Churf. g.

Vntertheniger

Gabriel Didymus

A Letter of Request from Gabriel Didymus to the Elector John Frederick

The mercy and peace of God be with you. Your Serene highborn Majesty, most gracious Lord, Your Royal Grace bestowed on me a donation for my house three years ago, for my wife and children. For this I do most humbly thank Your Royal Grace. I humbly inform Your Royal Grace that I have begun to build this very house and ask Your Royal Grace most humbly for a merciful donation, if Your Royal Grace most graciously pleases. I most humbly beg Your Royal Grace may not ungraciously perceive my request. Because I will owe very much, as the construction costs me more than was charged at first. The mercy of God be with Your Royal Grace and graciously maintain Your Royal Grace for us. Amen.

Your Royal Grace's
obedient
Gabriel Didymus

The Feud of Wurzen and the Departure of the Armour-Clad Vigilantes

The armour-clad vigilantes of Torgau in the past and present

BY DIETER MITTAG

The traditional coat of arms of the Torgau armour-clad vigilantes

The Torgau armour-clad vigilantes are first mentioned in a treaty of alliance of 1344 in fighting gangs and bandits between the towns of Torgau, Oschatz and Grimma. It virtually consisted of all citizens of Torgau that were obliged by town order to the purchase of helmet, harness and weapons and to regular arms training. In 1542 Elector John Frederick, who resided at Torgau, wanted to force the Bishopric of Meissen to pay the "Türkensteuer", a tax inducted by the Emperor for the defence against the Turks. The bishop of Meissen refused to pay. The Elector had the Torgau vigilantes mobilised without hesitation in order to occupy the closest town of the bishopric: Wurzen. The armour-clad troop of 128 men – more could not be assembled in the hurry – captured Wurzen on 22nd March without fighting. The Torgau men were followed by contingents from the Electorate of Saxony. However, Duke Maurice in Dresden regarded it as a gross defiance of his rights as co-regent and marched out against his electoral cousin with 10,000 footmen and 500 troopers. But there was no fight. Firm words of Martin Luther and the mediation by Landgrave Philip of Hesse made for the peaceful withdrawal of the troops. At Easter 1542, the Torgau armour-clad vigilantes returned to Torgau unscathed. They were treated with Osterfladen (Easter cake) everywhere along the way (which is why the event is humorously called "Fladenkrieg", which literally means "cake war"). In appreciation of their efforts, the Elector granted those involved the right to celebrate an annual commemorative festival. From 1824 onwards, this departure festival was only celebrated every two years. By then it had become the greatest folk festival of the region.

The members of the association in their traditional Renaissance garments, together with the mayor of Torgau. Assembling on the parade square before the parade, and the mounted armour-clad vigilantes

This would continue until 1938. During World War II, the festivals were cancelled, and at the end of the war the US soldiers took the armours from the castle along as war loot. The "Geharnischte Bürger-Compagnie" (armour-clad citizen company) was prohibited and the weapons and armaments left were passed to the museum.

The "Torgauer Geharnischtenverein e. V." (Association of the Armour-Clad Vigilantes of Torgau) was re-founded in 1990 in order to maintain the tradition. On this basis, the departure festival could also be revived, and after a difficult time of tireless development work, the first one could be organised in 1994. Since then it has been taking place every two years, as before, fascinating numerous spectators. The highlights of the festival are the coronation of the "Great King", who is determined in a competition in which the participants shoot a crossbow at a wooden eagle, the great parade from the market square to the grounds of the association together with other clubs and associations, and the festival polonaise of the armour-clad vigilantes.

The Torgau armour-clad vigilantes with their colourful Renaissance uniforms that are supplemented with harnesses on special occasions, are still welcome everywhere at festivals and parades. A special highlight in the association's history was the participation in the famous Steuben Parade in New York in 1997.

The association has about 100 active and passive members at the moment, who are committed to tradition. It divides into the armour-clad footmen and the mounted armour-clad vigilantes; the women form their own procession of sutler women.

In 2011, the show fight group "Faust Luthers" (fist of Luther) with an associated bivouac group was eventually founded. Their shared objective is to create a vivid and military-historically authentic representation of the Reformation age, first of all by presenting contemporary combat styles and bivouacs. Their repertoire contains everything from duels with batons, thrusting weapons, pikes and halberds right through to unarmed combat and the presentation of military bivouac life at Renaissance times. ●

▶ **DIETER MITTAG**
is the chairman of the Torgauer Geharnischtenverein e. V.

Beauty and Intellect

A Historic Prayer Book

The Torgau town archive contains a true treasure of Torgau printing art. It is a prayer book, which was printed in silver type at the *Herzoglich-Sächsische Officin* (ducal Saxon printing workshop) at Hartenfels Castle in 1596. Back then, the Administrator of the Saxon Electorate Friedrich Wilhelm I of Saxe-Weimar resided in Torgau. The text frames, each consisting of eight little woodcuts depicting scenes of the Old Testament, are of special importance: They represent a symbol of skilled printing work at the end of the 16th century. The more than 200 scenes are regularly repeated throughout the book's nearly 400 pages. Also worth mentioning are the little woodcut medallions at the bottom of each page showing, among others, the Reformer Martin Luther, his friend Philipp Melanchthon from Wittenberg and the Evangelists St. Matthew (as angel), St. Mark (as winged lion), St. Luke (as winged Taurus) and St. John (as eagle). The prayer book has a binding of carefully-tanned pigskin, probably dating back to the 17th century. Even though the title page of the work was not preserved, this prayer book can still be considered as a valuable enrichment of the town archive.

▶ www.torgau.eu

▶ **ANGELIKA GRÄBER**
is the former director of the Torgau town archive.

The Torgau History Association – Home to Museums and Regional History

The Torgau History Association succeeds the Torgau Antiquity Association, which was founded 130 years ago. It primarily took over the mission to maintain regional history and operate museums in the town. The association was founded in 1990 and has 80 members by now. It is the spiritual father of the Torgau Museum Path with seven museums at public and private sites of the historic centre. Furthermore, the association has so far presented remarkable regional-historic research results in 29 publications. The association's programme includes lecture events, conferences and excursions on the one hand, and operating vivid museums, collecting and maintaining despite dwindling resources on the other.

▶ www.museum-torgau.de

▶ **JÜRGEN HERZOG**

1 Stadt- und Kulturgeschichtliches Museum Torgau, Electoral Chancellery (▶ p. 59)
2 Lapidarium
3 Watchman Tower (▶ p. 78)
4 Brewery Museum with Brewery Vault and Brewery Cellar (▶ p. 10)
5 Mayor Ringenhain House (▶ p. 11)
6 Workman House (▶ p. 10)
7 Katharina Luther Parlour (▶ p. 51)

The Torgau Museum Path – Unique in Saxony

It all started back in 1993, when the Torgau History Association's vision of a series of museum highlights in the historic centre of the town was born. Much has happened since then. Allies were made, the Torgau Town Council paved the way and identified itself with the objectives. The museum of cultural and town history "Stadt- und Kulturgeschichtliches Museum" could be opened in 2005 at the house of the Electoral Chancellery – the birth place of the "chancellery language of Saxony", the German standard language of Martin Luther – after it had been extensively restored as a monument. Now, places of interest are threaded through Torgau, fascinating the interested visitor. Where once the watchman mounted guard on the Elector's sleep in the castle, on the Watchman Tower, the tourist can now enjoy spectacular views over Torgau. At the Elector's lounge you can experience original stone sculptures, architectural sculptures and construction history inside today's Lapidarium. The building in which Katharina Luther spent the final days of her life now houses the Katharina Luther Parlour. Representing the town's bread, brewing history is described in Wolf Giersing's Brewery Museum on Fischerstraße. The most splendid Renaissance residence in Saxony, the Mayor Ringenhain House, surprises with its carefully restored interior and allows an interesting insight into the bourgeois lifestyle at the time. However, the smallest property along the Museum Path is a very special gem indeed – the Workman House at the wall, a tiny, crooked building, which once hosted chimney sweepers and servants.

Those who only pay a short visit to Torgau and don't get to see all that simply have to return, otherwise they have never really been here.

▶ www.museum-torgau.de

▶ **JÜRGEN HERZOG**

The Rosery at Hartenfels Castle

The Torgau rosery was laid out more than 450 years ago, between 1534 and 1542, following the strict Renaissance-style principles.

There are large lawns in the lower part of the garden, which contrast nicely with small trees, shrubs and flowerbeds, completed with small trick fountains and sculptures.

At the beginning of the 16th century, an additional electoral herb and flower garden was laid out. However, its exact location is not traceable any more. But tradition has it that Augustus, Elector of Saxony (1526, Elector 1553–1586), was especially interested in botany. Therefore he asked Johannes Kentmann, a famous physician and naturalist, to write a herbal book for his private library.

The oldest historical source on this topic, the "plan of the castle buildings and gardens in Torgau", probably dates back to 1784. According to this plan, the gardens were divided into three parts: the rosery, which still exists today, the "Paradise" garden and the racecourse, also called tournament garden. The castle gardens, which were added to today's rosery, are still being bounded by two buildings, the Elbe magazine and the salt magazine. Both buildings are from the 18th century.

The rosery at the castle was extensively restored from 2000 until 2002. In doing so, the natural stone walls, the old stairways and the different terraces were revealed. A nuanced arrangement of plants now results in a perfect overall composition of the gardens. Today's ensemble includes harmoniously matching items of decoration and furniture like the sandstone fountains, a water basin in the terrace area, seating groups along with a wrought-iron pavilion, and beautiful garden benches.

▶ www.tic-torgau.de

▶ **CORNELIA KÖNIG**
is a cultural scientist and works as director of the museum of cultural and town history "Stadt- und Kulturgeschichtliches Museum Torgau".

Claus Narr – the Owlglass of the Electoral Court

In the late Middle Ages, jesters were an inherent part of court residences and enhanced the cultural life there. They were a special kind of servants, but occupied a privileged position. External characteristics of their "speciality" were physical handicaps and madness.

It was a fashion at that time that the ruler employed one or more "abnormal" people for general amusement. In most cases they led a quite comfortable life as they received lodging, clothes and food and were given astonishing leeway by their masters – the proverbial fool's licence.

However, only few were honoured in literary and artistic works. Claus Narr was one of them, because the electoral "all-round entertainer" amused the Ernestine Electors at their court for more than 75 years, publicly combining his comedy with repartee and candour. His jokes were well-known among the court members and are recorded today in a book of folk tales. Beyond that, there is a three-dimensional representation of Claus Narr in the form of a corbel figure on the right side of the Wendelstein staircase at Hartenfels Castle.

▶ www.tic-torgau.de

▶ **CORNELIA KÖNIG**

The Nativity, altar relief from the former abbey, around 1500, detail

The Museum of Cultural and Town History "Stadt- und Kulturgeschichtliches Museum" at the Electoral Chancellery

The Electorate of Saxony was a model of exemplary state administration. As the central Chancellery had its headquarters in Torgau and the "Old Chancellery" had become too small, Elector Frederick the Wise bought a building in the cloister garth from Nimbschen convent in 1523. In the 18th century, the building was used as "Manufactur in der Cantzelley" (manufactory at the Chancellery) for the production of fine woollen cloths. In 1711, Tsar Peter I visited Torgau to attend his son's wedding, and met the scholar Gottfried Wilhelm Leibniz.

The building of the "New Chancellery" with its large office, the document vaults and the council room has been housing the "Stadt- und Kulturgeschichtliche Museum" and its collection of town-historical artefacts since 2005. In the exhibition, Torgau's fate full of vicissitudes can be tracked from the pre- and ancient history to the present. A special treat are the Niese Room – a collection of items owned by a family in the 18th and 19th century, including a complete archive – and the Loebner Room, housing the collection of the oldest toy store.

▶ www.museum-torgau.de

▶ **JÜRGEN HERZOG UND KATHRIN NIESE**

Council trophy made by goldsmith Andreas Klette, 1599

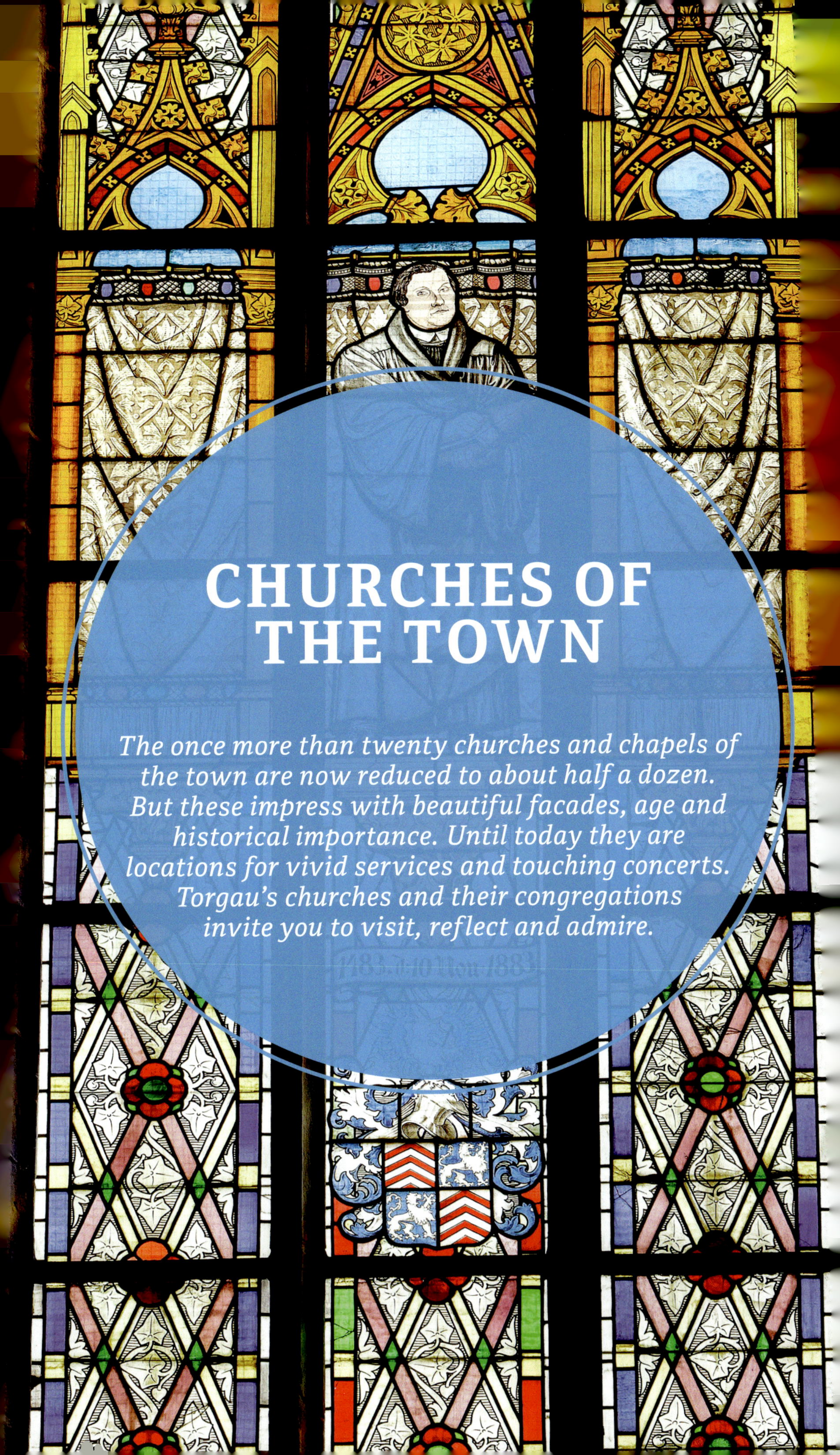

CHURCHES OF THE TOWN

The once more than twenty churches and chapels of the town are now reduced to about half a dozen. But these impress with beautiful facades, age and historical importance. Until today they are locations for vivid services and touching concerts. Torgau's churches and their congregations invite you to visit, reflect and admire.

"Solomon himself has never built a temple as beautiful as the one in Torgau."

About Martin Luther's special relationship with the churches of Torgau, in which the Reformation comes to life at authentic places

BY HANS CHRISTIAN BEER

No matter from which direction you may approach the old residence town of Torgau, you will always be greeted by its towers from afar. They define the skyline of this place. Apart from the three towers of the impressive Renaissance castle, the bell-bearing towers are dominant. Especially those of the Protestant St. Marien town church and the Nikolaikirche welcome the visitor from afar.

Churches have always been important reference points. Their purpose may have changed, which is what happened to the Nikolaikirche and the Alltagskirche (former abbey). But the public remains aware of their impact, as they still play an important role in town life. This includes, above all, the purpose for which churches were initially built: to praise God and console the people. In this frantic world, churches are places of reflection and recovery. Fear and terror, but also gratefulness and joy can be expressed here. Churches are open to everyone, no matter whether they come out of curiosity, for silent prayer or to attend a concert or service. Churches are welcoming places which link past and present.

St. Marien Town Church

The huge late Gothic nave of the venerable St. Marien town church towers above the town like a protective mother. When approaching this impressive building from the marketplace, the visitor first observes the mighty westwork with the two towers of different heights. This staunch building features stylistic elements from all its construction phases; from Romantic via Gothic, Renaissance and Baroque through to Rococo. The latter is represented by the southern tower, which was re-erected in 1750 in contemporary style after the fire disaster of 1748, which had been caused by a lightning strike.

There is evidence that first Romanesque predecessor of St. Marien existed around 1100. The church was first mentioned in a document from 1119. A piece of timber from the wall of the northern tower was dendrochronologically investigated and also points to that time.

The old basilica was extended and reconstructed around 1200. The round-arched windows of the northern tower and of the centre of the westwork date back to this time.

When the visitor then enters the wide late Gothic nave, passing through the 800-year-old barrel-

The predella of the high altar: "Abendmahl" (the Lord's Supper) by Johann Heinrich Sperling, 1698

◀ P. 62
The alabaster baptismal font at St. Marien, sponsored by pharmacist and councilman Gottfried Kistenmacher, 1693, and the pulpit made by Georg Wittenberger, 1582

◀ P. 60/61
The pulpit of the Castle Chapel from 1544 and a stained glass picture of St. Marien town church

Mass at the Catholic church "Zur Schmerzhaften Mutter Gottes" (Dolorous Mother of God) (▶ P. 69)

▶ P. 65
Started in 1543 by Nickel Gromann, the Castle Chapel was consecrated in 1544 by Martin Luther as the first Protestant church construction

vaulted hallway, he will be impressed with its size and brightness. Especially on sunny days the light floods into the interior through the numerous high windows. The nave and aisles have about the same height and are separated by slim columns that seem to reach for the sky. The construction of this hall began in the first half of the 14th century. It was finished around 1500 and stood the test of time until today.

However, little of the original medieval equipment is left. Apart from some exposed mural paintings, a wing of the Gothic main altar reminds of pre-Reformation times. But the most prominent testimony of this epoch is the sepulchral monument of Duchess Sophie of Mecklenburg. It was cast in 1504 at the Vischer workshop in Nuremberg and depicts Frederick the Wise's sister in law, who had died young. In connection with this grave, an altar for Saint Anne and the Fourteen Holy Helpers was donated. It was painted by Lucas Cranach the Elder. One picture from this altar showing the Fourteen Holy Helpers survived until today.

During the crucial years of the Reformation, the town church was a sermon church of the electoral court and the citizens of Torgau. Martin Luther himself often preached from the pulpit. The Reformer's wife Katharina von Bora also found her last resting place within these walls after her death on 20th December 1552. She is still being memorised by her impressive gravestone, which features her in a life-size image. In the course of the Reformation, the church was fundamentally re-designed. The 16 medieval altars that existed by then were removed and renovations in Baroque style were carried out. The high altar and the baptismal font date back to that time.

The latest fitment is the organ, which was installed in 1984 by Schuster, an organ building company in Zittau. It is a symbol of the importance of this church for church music, as it was the "first cantor" Johann Walter's place of activity. He played his music with the boys' and citizens' choirs on the southern gallery.

Throughout the centuries, St. Marien town church has remained the place of worship of the Torgau parish. It is where Christians celebrate church service, children and adults are baptised, teenagers are confirmed and couples get married.

Castle Chapel

The Protestant congregation of Torgau has a second church. During the cold season between October and Pentecost, the church community meets at the Castle Chapel, which is an especially prominent construction that reminds of Reformation and church renewal in an impressive way. Reformation can be experienced at first hand in this building. The Torgau Castle Chapel is regarded as the first new church construction that was planned and completed from scratch in accordance with Protestant principles. It was consecrated by Martin Luther in 1544. The Roman Catholic consecration ritual

The Torgau Castle Chapel was the first construction that was planned, built and consecrated fully in the spirit of the Reformation. Luther himself held the first sermon here in 1544.

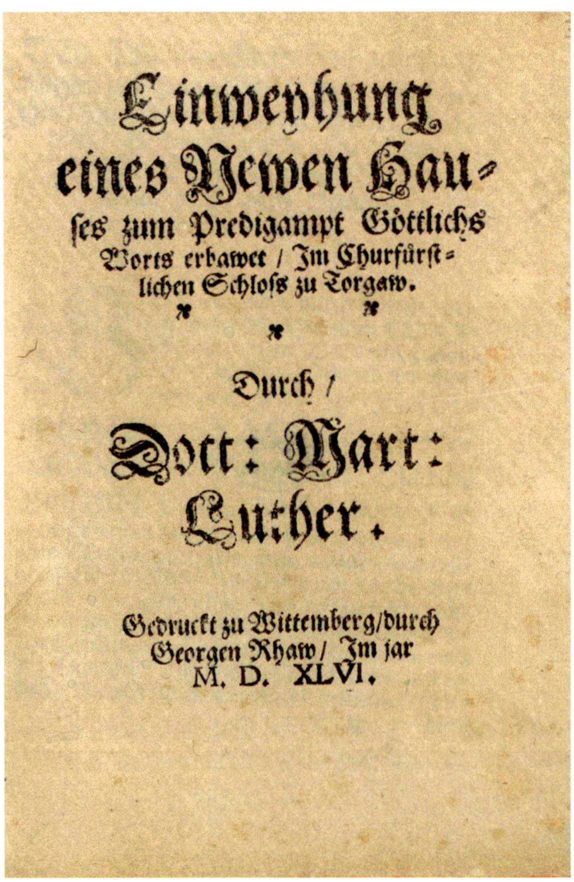
Einweyhung
eines Newen Hau-
ses zum Predigampt Göttlichs
Worts erbawet / Im Churfürst-
lichen Schlos zu Torgaw.

Durch /
Doct: Mart:
Luther.

Gedruckt zu Wittemberg/durch
Georgen Rhaw/ Im jar
M. D. XLVI.

The sermon preached by Martin Luther at the consecration on 5th October 1544, printed in 1546 in Wittenberg by Georg Rhau

that was common up until then did no longer apply. Luther himself said in his consecration sermon on 5th October 1544: *For it to be rightly and Christianly consecrated and blessed, we will begin to hear the word of God and act in accordance with it. … And now that you, my dear friends, helped to sprinkle it with the right holy water of the word of God, help me carry the thurible as well, that is pray …*

Coming from the courtyard through the decorated portal rich in figures, the visitor enters the clearly-structured church interior where the depiction of the Arms of Christ reminds him of Luther's *theologia crucis*. The high, plain interior is structured by the two galleries, which are extensions of the storeys of the adjacent buildings.

Only few items from the original equipment survived. One of them is the decorated pulpit, which is the first thing that catches the visitor's eye on entering the room. It was created by the stone sculptor Simon Schröter, and its images show central points of the new Protestant theology. *Sola gratia, sola scriptura, sola fide, solus Christus* are illustrated in different Bible scenes: Christ and the adulteress, 12-year-old Jesus at the temple, the cleansing of the temple and the baptism of Jesus, which unfortunately got lost.

The free-standing table of the altar, which is borne by four angels, was reconstructed after its destruction at the end of World War II. The Reformation changed the relation to saints. Relics were no longer worshipped and therefore were not thematised on Protestant altars any more. Instead, people focussed on the communal celebration of the Eucharist.

An especially beautiful piece of artwork is the dedication plaque cast by bronze founder Hilger at the Saxon town of Freiberg. It contains a poem praising this church, its constructors and Luther himself.

The organ, which was installed recently in 1994, was made based on ancient models. It symbolises the great significance of church music in Protestantism. Johann Walter for example, Luther's friend and first Protestant cantor, composed a psalm motet especially for the chapel's consecration.

The former Franciscan abbey (Alltagskirche), the construction of which was sponsored by the elector, around 1496–1513

Alltagskirche

A place that reminds of the negative side effects of Reformation events is the former Franciscan abbey. On Ash Wednesday on 25th March 1525, furious Torgau citizens stormed the Franciscan monastery, beat up the monks and destroyed the church furniture and equipment.

This rage settled in the subsequent years. The abbey became property of the town and, at the recommendation of Luther, was used for weekly service by the Torgau congregation. The monastery was probably founded around 1240, soon after the Franciscan order had been approved by the Pope in 1210. A first abbey and the monastery buildings were erected in the 1340s. Today's abbey is a new construction from the end of the 15th and the beginning of the 16th century. In post-Reformation times, this building served other, very different purposes, until it eventually was used by the secondary school after World War I. The church was later transformed into a gym, and in 1997 it became the school hall of the Johan-Walter-Gymnasium, after it had been extensively restored.

Nikolaikirche

Somewhat hidden in the court of the Town Hall is another church which is relevant for the Reformation. Its towers also shape the townscape, and its bells are an integral part of the peal which can be heard three times a day.

The Nikolaikirche has not been used as a church since the 1630s. Up until then it had been the parish church of the merchants' settlement, and its foundation dates back to the early 13th century.

In the years of the Lutheran Reformation, the Nikolaikirche was the main gathering place of the new religious movement. The preacher at St. Nikolai, Dominican Friar Valentin Tham, already baptised children using the German language as early as 1519. In 1520 he confessed to Luther's theology in his preaches. Justus Jonas preached here in 1525. Catholic masses have not been held in this church since 1526. At the Torgau visitation of 1529, the church was already unneeded and sealed. According to the visitation report it was passed to the Council for alternative usage.

So it was used as a store and for economical purposes after the Reformation, and from the 17th century onwards only as a warehouse and a prison. In

the 19th century, it was the administration and prison cell building of the District and Land Court of Torgau.

Presently there is a more or less intense consideration of restoring and reconstructing the existing leftovers of the building in order to give them a new purpose.

Catholic Church

It is the parish church of the Catholic congregation and bears the Name “Zur Schmerzhaften Mutter Gottes” (Dolorous Mother of God). From 1850 onwards, a Catholic mission and parish have existed in Torgau. In 1855, a church was built next to the inn “Zum Goldenen Löwen” (golden lion) in front of the former baker’s gate, which unfortunately burnt down in 1906. The new construction from 1908 was basically modelled on the medieval Romanesque churches containing a nave, a transept, low side naves and a choir. Since the consecration, the choir has been housing a three-part high altar decorated with different mosaics and reliefs depicting the Nativity at Bethlehem and the Resurrection of Christ. The central mosaic contains the image of a pelican feeding its starving young ones with its heart’s blood. The windows above the high altar show scenes of Saint Mary’s life. Two side altars depict Saint George killing a dragon with his lance on the left, and Mother Mary weeping for her dead son Jesus on the right.

New Apostolic Church

The congregation of the New Apostolic Church has been existing in Torgau for a little more than a hundred years. In 2008 the construction of a community hall was started at No. 8, Naundorfer Straße. It could be consecrated in the following year. With this the congregation received a new church, which is located close to the old one and meets all requirements of a modern church building as well as those of urban designing. It provides room for nearly 300 visitors. Apart from the church hall along with its gallery, the building features several side rooms with various options for use. ●

▶ **HANS CHRISTIAN BEER**
is a Protestant pastor in Torgau.

The new church building is a bright and open meeting place for the members of the Torgau congregation of the New Apostolic church. Service and musical engagement in the choir and orchestra are especially important for an active congregational life

◀ P. 68
The so-called “Bischofsmützen” (bishops’ caps), the towers of the Romanesque Nikolaikirche, greet the visitors of the town from afar. Immediately after the secularisation in 1529, it was used as a cloth hall, store, court building and as flour scales, among others

The "Peaceful Revolution" in Torgau

Excerpts from the diary of Matthias Grimm-Over, youth officer of the Protestant church district of Torgau in 1989 and co-founder and district spokesman of the Torgau New Forum until 2nd October 1990

BY MATTHIAS GRIMM-OVER

Sunday, 8th October 1989
60 citizens of Torgau meet spontaneously at the Protestant community hall at No. 22, Leipziger Straße. Planned are the communication of information on the new political groups and the discussion of the establishment of a citizens' forum in Torgau. Surprised by the great interest, we arrange weekly Sunday meetings at the town church.

In the course of the event, the state forces turn up! Policemen with dogs patrol Leipziger Straße and check passers-by. A truck with armed trainees of the Dommitzsch People's Police Academy stops in front of the district administration office of the People's Police. The district council's representative for church affairs confronts us outside the community hall with the threat: "You're not getting out!" Reason wins in the end, and all attenders of our meeting are allowed to leave or climb over backyard walls, taking flyers with them.

Sunday, 22nd October 1989
Meanwhile we are more than a thousand people at the Sunday prayers for the renewal of the town church. The open microphone gets ever more popular. People speak freely and confidently at this historic Reformation site. More and more come to our campaigns outside the church walls. The New Forum has organised, and my large apartment at the Superintendenture serves as office and information centre. Flyers are produced now in my living room, and the many helpers are catered for in the kitchen. My bedroom is my last safe haven.

Tuesday, 7th November 1989
After the New Forum has been working for three weeks now, I can spare some time to help founding the Social Democratic Party of the GDR. I act as meeting chairman in the backroom of a Torgau traditional pub and help the "Genossen"

(comrades) with the set-up. Of course no one wants to be called Genosse.

Wednesday, 8th November 1989
Even the CDU (Christian Democratic Union) of the East has read the signs of the times now and carries through a first citizens' forum at the Kreiskulturhaus (arts centre of the GDR). As representative of the New Forum, I am greeted with a smile. The party base revolts against the bloc parties, and I gladly join in.

Thursday, 9th November 1989
After some spontaneous campaigns, the first planned demonstration takes place. All streets around the town church are packed with people an hour before the actual start. We peacefully approach the market square. They say that eight thousand people were there in the end. I couldn't estimate a crowd like that. After the demonstration, we introduce the New Forum at the Cultural Association, and in the evening some good friends from Halle bring some news. Somewhere inbetween, the Berlin Wall falls, and in our hustle and bustle we don't even notice.

Tuesday, 5th December 1989
The district offices of the Stasi are occupied. Together with a pastor, a doctor and a workman, I decide to try something similar in Torgau. Together with the district's state prosecutor, we seal the rooms of the district office of the Stasi and of the SED's (Socialist Unity Party of Germany) district committee. The "party's sword and shied" sanctimoniously surrenders to our small group, or rather plays a game on us idealists.
Behind our backs, they continue to shred documents and money and weapons are stashed away. The Genossen seem to discover capitalism after all. While we idealists are still fighting for a reformation of society with candles in our hands, the first business concepts have already been developed, and the eyes are firmly on the necessary properties along with the respective houses. Tough luck, Karl Marx!

Friday, 22nd December 1989
Plenary meeting of the New Forum at the metal workers' house. The political interests divaricate increasingly. Some want a party, others a citizen movement. Some want a reformed GDR, others a united fatherland. I won't be able to hold this bunch together for long. The events overrun our thinking – Merry Christmas!

Addition

Tuesday, 2nd October 1990
In the evening we dissolve the Torgau New Forum. After almost a year of intensive work we conclude our project without melancholy – but very burnt-out indeed. We all need a break now and finally treat ourselves to a beer on the Torgau market square, where the high-spirited public celebrates the eve of the German Reunification in a marquee. The first verse of the German national anthem is shouted into my ears, and I prefer to go to bed. I sleep the dawning of the new age away. ●

▶ **MATTHIAS GRIMM-OVER**
is a social pedagogue and works as consultant for child's and youth work at the Protestant church district of Torgau and Delitzsch.

Demonstration on 9th November 1989 in Torgau

Prayer for reformation in October 1989 at St. Marien

The author of the text, Matthias Grimm-Over, on the microphone

The Church and the Town

BY HANS CHRISTIAN BEER

Protestant Town Cemetery

In the course of Torgau's development as fortress at the beginning of the 19th century, the old cemetery had to be abandoned and a new one was laid out. This happened in 1811. The mortal remains of more than 200 decedents were transferred. Then the new cemetery on Dommitzscher Straße was inaugurated on 24th March 1811 with the funeral of 20-year-old Cannoneer Corporal of the Royal Saxon Field Artillery Regiment Carl Johann Schneider. Some valuable gravestones from the previous 200 years can be seen and are part of the town's history. At the beginning of the 20th century, the cemetery hall was erected in discreet art-nouveau style. It was renovated for the 200th anniversary of the cemetery and offers all mourners a dignified setting for saying a last farewell to their loved ones.

Friends' Association "Förderverein Stadtkirche St. Marien e. V."

What would a church be without its congregation? Torgau's Protestant congregation has more than 2,000 members and is an inherent part of the town's public life. It invites people to come to masses, concerts and a variety of other events. In doing so, it does not only address local believers, but also everyone else who might be interested. Apart from acting as cultural medium, it looks after social concerns. The Christians of the congregation work closely with the Protestant charitable organisation "Diakonisches Werk Torgau-Oschatz", which is the provider of a nursery school and an ambulant ecumenical hospice, among others.

The deeply committed friend's association "Stadtkirche St. Marien e. V." is responsible for the preservation of the church buildings in possession or under administration of the congregation. In the light of the upcoming 500th anniversary of the Reformation, it is especially important to present the Castle Chapel and the Town Church to the numerous visitors in a good condition. The Torgau Protestant congregation would like to welcome them to its churches with open arms and appear as a good host.

▶ www.evkirchetorgau.de/gemeinde/foerderverein

Charitable Organisation “Diakonisches Werk Torgau-Oschatz”

In the context of the Reformation, a new system of care of the poor and needy had to be introduced. As congregation and civic community were not distinguished, this task fell to the Council. However, in the following centuries it was deliberately seen as a specific scope of Christian congregations. Going back to Johann Hinrich Wichern, diaconal associations and aid organisations were set up everywhere. According to the motto “helping with words and deeds”, the Protestant charitable organisation “Diakonisches Werk Torgau-Oschatz” helps the socially weak, the needy and people in difficult living situations right where help is needed. The work is done professionally in a very special way, and its guidelines are in accordance with the Christian policy of the service to the people.

From 1990 onwards, diaconal organisations were founded as state and local associations in East Germany. Just like the diaconal organisation in the church district of Torgau and the diaconal organisation of the Evangelical-Lutheran Church of Saxony in the church district of Oschatz. Together, these two associations founded the non-profit limited company “Evangelisches Diakoniewerk Oschatz-Torgau” on 1st January 1998. They aimed at combining the work of the social consultant services and institutions of both associations in a common sponsorship. A special focus of work is on pregnancy and addiction counselling as well as on an ambulant hospice and assisted living for mentally chronically ill singles and couples. In addition to that, there is a teenager migration service and a psycho-social contact point and counselling service, as well as socio-pedagogical family assistance and, beyond that, a Protestant nursery school called “Sonnenschein” (sunshine).

▶ www.diakonie-oschatz-torgau.de

Protestant Youth Education Project “wintergrüne”

Among the many other impressive Renaissance houses of our town, the house at No. 2, Wintergrüne, is of special significance. Here, the first Superintendenture was established in 1529. In a parlour on the building’s ground floor, the reformers Luther, Melanchthon, Bugenhagen and Jonas handed the Articles of Torgau to Elector John the Steadfast at the end of March 1530. These articles would later become the base of the Augsburg Confession.

From 2005 onwards, the Protestant youth education project has been offering activities for confirmees and students of religion and ethics classes. Under the slogan “Roots and Wings”, teenagers can deal with the world of morality and develop their own moral values. They find stimulations for this in a multimedia exhibition. The young and old visitors can inform themselves of the Reformation and try to make connections between the past and the present at a large multimedia wall.

▶ www.wintergruene.de

ATTRACTIONS AND SIGHTS

A pilgrimage on the Luther Way, the magnificent view from the Watchman Tower, exciting tours of the town and of course, the long-standing breeding of noble horses in Graditz stud in the Elbe meadows – Torgau and its surroundings invite to explore a range of attractions.

Torgau/Elbe – Been Here Yet?

A tour of the town guided by women

Three women who could not be more different, invite to guided tours. They appear in historic robes and never get tired of raving about the beauty of Torgau's buildings. "He who enters matrimony enters a monastery full of spiritual crises" is what Martin Luther said. But Katharina would not have been "Mister Käthe" had she not had an answer to that.

The baker's wife Sophie guides through the historic centre, telling about her life, and the master, of course. She even knows where the Dresden Stollen comes from.

There are many mills around Torgau. The miller sent Lieschen to town all alone. Together with her, you'll see houses of simple, but also of well-heeled citizens and even the castle with totally different eyes. ●

▶ **Bookings and information via:**
Torgau Information Centre, Markt 1, 04860 Torgau,
Telephone: +49 (0)3421 70140, Fax: +49 (0)3421 701415
www.tic-torgau.de

On Horseback

A brief history of Graditz Principal Stud

Elector John George III founded the Torgau Studs in 1686. In this network of outlying estates and farms which had already been developed as farms, Repitz near Torgau and Graditz had a prominent role. When his son Augustus I took over the studs, he engaged the architect to the Saxon court, Matthäus Daniel Pöppelmann, to expand Graditz. The stud park, which was built between 1720 and 1725, fits well into the Baroque stud grounds. Its three lime tree alleys are arranged in a star-shape and lead up to Graditz Castle. The main alley, also called Torgau Alley, is a visual axis to Hartenfels Castle and St. Marien church in Torgau. Situated in the centre of the park, near the castle, are an art-historically interesting horse sculpture and the baroque pavilion, which is also referred to as the Teahouse.

The Royal Saxon Stud in Graditz served as a supplier of horses for the residence in Dresden. The horses that were bred here were used in par force hunting, which was a trend at the time, for the military, but also as carriage horses of the Elector, who also reigned in Warsaw as King of Poland. Hence, more than 500 horses were kept at the hitch up stations which had been set up for him along the road from Dresden to Poland. The Torgau Studs only received a real breeding function at the turn of the 19th century, when the Saxon studs first began to keep breeding stallions.

As a result of the Napoleonic Wars of Liberation, the territory which was passed to Prussia after the Congress of Vienna in 1815 included Saxony's most important stud farms. From 1845 to 1890, the Prussian Stud Administration had the stables in the inner courtyard, the summer stables in the Elbe meadows and the paddocks (a special environment for foal rearing) in the park restored or constructed. The copestones of the stable buildings bear witness to the various construction periods and sovereigns.

After World War II, the stud was under Soviet administration and became subject to agrarian reform. The stud's herds were all passed to the Soviet Union: The Thoroughbreds along with the 250-year-old stud records went to Voskhod Stud Farm, and the horses which had been evacuated from Trakehnen Principal Stud in 1944 went to Kirov Stud Farm.

In 1949, Graditz was re-established as publicly owned Principal Stud, which bred racehorses from about 100 Thoroughbreds and also possessed a small herd of Trakehners for the production of stallions.

After the political situation in Germany had changed, the Saxon Stud Administration was established in 1992. Since then, all horse breeding tasks of Moritzburg State Stud, Graditz Principal Stud and the professional state school for riding and driving have been lying with the sovereignty of the Free State of Saxony. A mare herd of German Sport Horses is kept at Graditz Principal Stud, mainly for remount production for Moritzburg State Stud. Along with other services like rearing of young horses and keeping of brood mares for foaling, fully qualified grooms for keeping and service as well as for breeding are being trained here. In addition to that, the private breeding of Thoroughbreds is also established in Graditz, on the basis of a treaty.

The continuation of Graditz is a special concern to the Free State of Saxony, as it aims to pass on this tradition of horse breeding to following generations and to maintain its cultural heritage. ●

▶ **STEFFEN BOTHENDORF**
is a certified agricultural engineer and works as director of Graditz Principal Stud.

▶ www.saechsische-gestuetsverwaltung.de

Looking Down on Torgau's Rooftops

The Watchman Tower

The basically medieval, and with an impressive 53 metres highest tower of Hartenfels Castle is a link between the late Gothic Albrechtsbau (wing D) and the magnificent Early Renaissance Johan-Friedrich-Bau (wing C).

The enlargement and expansion of the Watchman Tower as well as the installation of the three-storey Italian-style loggia on the castle's courtyard side featuring delicate and imaginative sculptures was carried out between 1533 and 1535. This marked the beginning of one of the most ambitious and important undertakings of Elector John Frederick the Magnanimous: reconstructing the castle of Torgau. Once you have climbed the 163 steps of the winding stairs leading up to the tower's observation platform, you can enjoy the magnificent 360-degree view over Torgau's rooftops and the vast Elbe landscape. Inside the tower there are an interesting exhibition on the life of jester Hans Narr, who inhabited one of the tower's chambers around 1500, and a photo documentation of the Saxon hundred-year flood of 2002. Both are well worth the effort of climbing up.

▶ **CORNELIA KÖNIG**

The "Kulturbastion" in Torgau

The sociocultural centre "Kulturbastion" (bastion of culture) is known far beyond Torgau's borders. It is located in the former flank casemate of Bastion II, a distinctive element of the Saxon-Prussian Fortress of Torgau. The historical monument had been carefully restored, and was reopened in 2005 as a modern event centre and living history site. Culture is involved at full range: music, cinema, cabaret, media relations and film. Concerts, shows and readings with more or less famous artists, authors and bands are organised on a regular basis. Especially well-known German- or English-speaking bands have played here in recent years. The art house cinema is equipped with the latest Dolby 3D Digital Cinema technique and mainly screens international films. The operator of the Kulturbastion is the non-profit association "KAP – Kulturelles Aktionsprojekt Torgau e. V." (cutural initiative project), which is responsible for program planning, technics, gastronomy and youth work.

▶ www.kulturbastion.de

▶ **DR MICHAEL REINIGER**
is counsellor for culture and tourism of the Torgau town administration.

The Luther Way in Saxony

A journey through 500 years of change characterized by the Reformation

Luther and Katharina in the Döbeln church Nikolaikirche

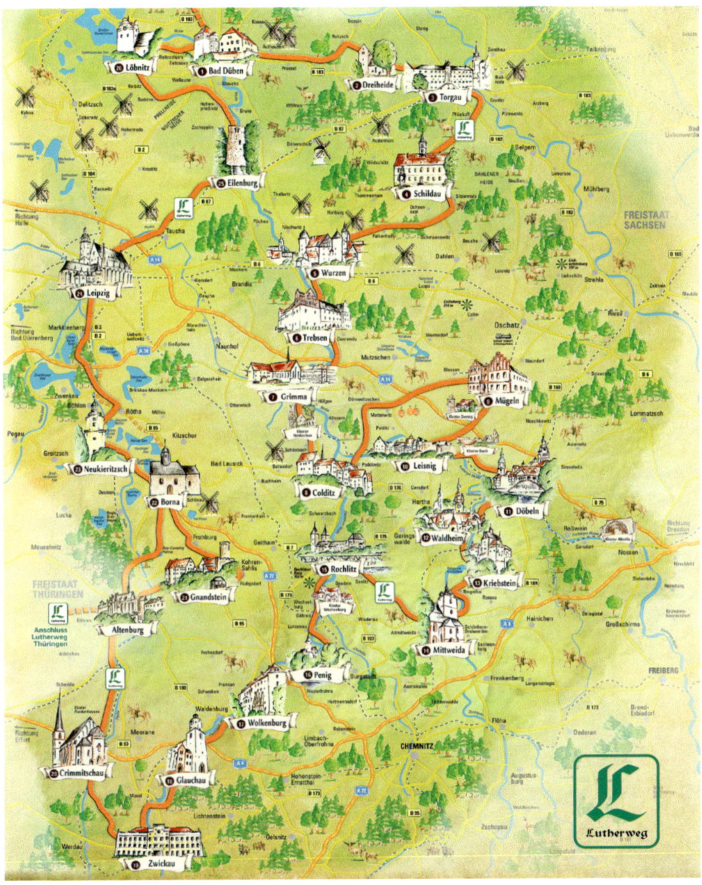

The church in Loebnitz

It's nice to free ourselves from daily stress. Walking the Luther Way is a great opportunity for this. The 550-kilometre spiritual circular walk passes through the beautiful landscapes of the Saxon Heath, the Saxon Burgenland and the Leipzig Neuseenland, inviting you to visit the Reformation sites. Discover the marks the Reformation left in this historical landscape which is so rich in tradition. The Luther Way in Saxony links towns, sites and places at which Martin Luther and his companions worked. It forms a network with the other German Luther Ways and is connected to walks in Thuringia and Saxony Anhalt.

For further information please go to:
www.lutherweg-sachsen.de

TOURIST INFORMATIONS ALONG THE WAY

Leipzig Tourist Information
Katharinenstr. 8, 04109 Leipzig
Telephone: +49 (0)341 7104260
Mon – Fri 9:30 a.m. – 6 p.m.
Sat 9:30 a.m. – 4 p.m., Sun, bank holidays 9:30 a.m. – 3 p.m.
www.leipzig.travel

Eilenburg Town Information
Torgauer Straße 40,
04838 Eilenburg
Telephone: +49 (0)3423 652222
Tue – Fri 9 a.m. – 12 a.m. /
1 p.m. – 5 p.m.
Sat 9 a.m. – 3 p.m., Sun 10 a.m.–12 a.m. / 1 p.m. – 5 p.m.
www.eilenburg.de

Bad Düben Tourist Information
Neuhofstraße 3a,
04849 Bad Düben
Telephone: +49 (0)34243 52886
Mon – Fri 10 a.m. – 5 p.m.,
Sat 10 a.m. – 4 p.m.
www.bad-dueben.de

Torgau Information Centre
Markt 1, 04860 Torgau
Telephone: +49 (0)3421 70140
Mon – Fri 9 a.m. – 6 p.m.,
Sat, Sun, bank holidays
10 a.m. – 4 p.m.
www.tic-torgau.de

Schildau Tourist Information
Bahnhofstr. 17,
04889 Belgern-Schildau
Telephone: +49 (0)34221 50731
Tue 12 a.m. – 3 p.m.,
Thu 12 a.m. – 6 p.m.
www.belgernschildau.de

Wurzen Tourist Information
Domgasse 2, 04808 Wurzen
Telephone: +49 (0)3425 8560400
Mon – Fri 10 a.m. – 1 p.m. /
2 p.m. – 6 p.m.
Sat, Sun 11 a.m. – 4 p.m.
www.tourismus-wurzen.de

Grimma Town Information
Markt 3, 04668 Grimma
Telephone: +49 (0)3437 9858 285
Mon – Fri 10 a.m. – 6 p.m.,
Sat 10 a.m. – 4 p.m.
www.grimma.de

Leisnig Tourist Office
Kirchstr. 15, 04703 Leisnig
Telephone: +49 (0)34321 637090
Tue, Thu, Fri 10 a.m. – 12 a.m. /
1 p.m. – 4 p.m.
Sat, Sun 10 a.m. – 3 p.m.
www.leisnig.de

Döbeln Information
Obermarkt 1, 04720 Döbeln
Telephone: +49 (0)3431 579161
Mon – Fri 9:30 a.m. – 1 p.m. /
1:30 p.m. – 5:30 p.m.,
Sat 9 a.m. – 12 a.m.
www.doebeln.de

Masthead

TORGAU PLACES OF THE REFORMATION
Journal 16.1

Published by the town administration of Torgau
Editorial board: Hans Christian Beer, Axel Frey, Dr Jürgen Herzog, Dr Michael Reiniger

This publication will be listed by the German National Library in the German national bibliography; for detailed bibliographic information please go to http://dnb.ddb.de

Printed in EU-H 7894

IDEA TO THE SERIES
Thomas Maess, publicizer, and Johannes Schilling, Reformation historian

OUTLINE OF THE JOURNALS
Burkhard Weitz, Editor of the journal Chrismon

COVER DESIGN
NORDSONNE IDENTITY, Berlin

COVER PICTURE
Jörg Schöner, Dresden

LAYOUT
NORDSONNE IDENTITY, Berlin

IMAGE EDITORS
Axel Frey and Michael Reiniger

IMAGE EDITING
David Burghardt / dbphoto.de

ISBN 978-3-374-04133-6
www.eva-leipzig.de

AXEL FREY
Executive editor

AM ANFANG WAR DAS WORT
LUTHER 2017
500 JAHRE REFORMATION

www.luther2017.de

Image Credits

Hans Christian Beer: p. 72 bottom
Steffen Bothendorf: p. 74/75, 77
Erdmute and Manfred Bräunlich: p. 32 top, 70, 71
Dirk Brzoska: p. 14
Christoph Busse: p. 8/9, 17, 21, 22, 23, 61, 63, 68
The Cleveland Museum of Art: p. 36/37
Gemeinde Torgau der Neuapostolischen Kirche: p. 69
Gunther Emmerlich: p. 81
Evangelische Kindertagesstätte "Sonnenschein": p. 73 left
Evangelisches Jugendbildungsprojekt "wintergrüne": p. 73 right
Geheimes Staatsarchiv Preußischer Kulturbesitz Berlin: p. 24
Helmut Graul: p. 29
Antje Hainz: p. 46
Hauptstaatsarchiv Dresden: p. 30–35
Archiv Herzog: p. 10 top right, 10 bottom, p. 44 bottom, 47 top
Andreas Holfert: p. 59 bottom right
Allan Jackson: p. 34 bottom
Nordsonne: p. 15, 57, 72/73
Michael Reiniger: p. 19 top, 28, 41, 58, 67, 72, 78 bottom
Andreas Schmidt: p. 12/13, 18, 19 bottom, 20, 31, 51, 52, 59 top, 60, 62, 65, 78 top
Jörg Schöner: Cover Picture
Peter Schönpflug: p. 64
Wolfgang Sens: p. 76
Wolfgang Siesing: p. 79 bottom
Staatliche Kunstsammlungen Dresden: p. 25, 38, 39
Stadt- und Kulturgeschichtliches Museum Torgau: p. 10 top left, 11, 16, 26, 32/33, 47 bottom, 50, 56 bottom, 59 bottom left
Stadtarchiv Torgau: p. 42, 44, 48, 56 top
Stadtverwaltung Torgau: p. 1
Stiftung Luthergedenkstätten in SachsenAnhalt: p. 40 left, 40 right, 43, 53, 66
Thinkstock: p. 6/7
Torgauer Geharnischte e. V.: p. 54, 55
Tourismusverband "Sächsisches Burgen und Heideland" e. V.: p. 79 top
Ulbricht, Oliver: p. 4/5
Villeroy & Boch AG, Unternehmensarchiv: p. 33 top